ISBN 978-1-5276-9901-4
PIBN 10882080

1 MONTH OF
FREE
READING

at

www.ForgottenBooks.com

By purchasing this book you are eligible for one month membership to ForgottenBooks.com, giving you unlimited access to our entire collection of over 1,000,000 titles via our web site and mobile apps.

To claim your free month visit:

www.forgottenbooks.com/free882080

English
Français
Deutsche
Italiano
Español
Português

www.forgottenbooks.com

Mythology Photography **Fiction**
Fishing Christianity **Art** Cooking
Essays Buddhism Freemasonry
Medicine **Biology** Music **Ancient
Egypt** Evolution Carpentry Physics
Dance Geology **Mathematics** Fitness
Shakespeare **Folklore** Yoga Marketing
Confidence Immortality Biographies
Poetry **Psychology** Witchcraft
Electronics Chemistry History **Law**
Accounting **Philosophy** Anthropology
Alchemy Drama Quantum Mechanics
Atheism Sexual Health **Ancient History**
Entrepreneurship Languages Sport
Paleontology Needlework Islam
Metaphysics Investment Archaeology
Parenting Statistics Criminology
Motivational

FORS CLAVIGERA.

LETTERS

TO THE WORKMEN AND LABOURERS OF GREAT BRITAIN.

BY

JOHN RUSKIN, LL.D.,

HONORARY STUDENT OF CHRIST CHURCH, AND SLADE PROFESSOR OF FINE ART.

VOL. I.

GEORGE ALLEN,
SUNNYSIDE, ORPINGTON, KENT.
1871.

FORS CLAVIGERA.

FIRST SERIES.

CONTENTS OF VOL. I. (1871.)

FORS CLAVIGERA.

LETTER THE 1st.

LOOKING DOWN FROM INGLEBOROUGH.

DENMARK HILL,

FRIENDS, 1*st January*, 1871.

WE begin to-day another group of ten years, not in happy circumstances. Although, for the time, exempted from the direct calamities which have fallen on neighbouring states, believe me, we have not escaped them because of our better deservings, nor by our better wisdom ; but only for one or two bad reasons, or for both : either that we have not sense enough to determine in a great national quarrel which side is right, or that we have not courage to defend the right, when we have discerned it.

I believe that both these bad reasons exist in full force; that our own political divisions prevent us from understanding the laws of international justice ; and that, even if we did, we should not dare to defend, perhaps not even to assert them, being on this first of January, 1871, in much bodily fear ; that is to say, afraid of the Russians ;

1.]

afraid of the Prussians ; afraid of the Americans ; afraid of the Hindoos ; afraid of the Chinese ; afraid of the Japanese ; afraid of the New Zealanders ; and afraid of the Caffres : and very justly so, being conscious that our only real desire respecting any of these nations has been to get as much out of them as we could.

They have no right to complain of us, notwithstanding, since we have all, lately, lived ourselves in the daily endeavour to get as much out of our neighbours and friends as we could ; and having by this means, indeed, got a good deal out of each other, and put nothing into each other, the actually obtained result, this day, is a state of emptiness in purse and stomach, for the solace of which our boasted " insular position " is ineffectual.

I have listened to many ingenious persons, who say we are better off now than ever we were before. I do not know how well off we were before ; but I know positively that many very deserving persons of my acquaintance have great difficulty in living under these improved circumstances : also, that my desk is full of begging letters, eloquently written either by distressed or dishonest people ; and that we cannot be called, as a nation, well off, while so many of us are either living in honest or in villanous beggary.

For my own part, I will put up with this state of things, passively, not an hour longer. I am not an unselfish person, nor an Evangelical one ; I have no particular pleasure in doing good ; neither do I dislike doing it so much as to expect to be rewarded for it in another world.

But I simply cannot paint, nor read, nor look at minerals, nor do anything else that I like, and the very light of the morning sky, when there is any—which is seldom, now-a-days, near London—has become hateful to me, because of the misery that I know of, and see signs of, where I know it not, which no imagination can interpret too bitterly.

Therefore, as I have said, I will endure it no longer quietly; but henceforward, with any few or many who will help, do my poor best to abate this misery.   But that I may do my best, I must not be miserable myself any longer ; for no man who is wretched in his own heart, and feeble in his own work, can rightly help others.

Now my own special pleasure has lately been con-nected with a given duty.   I have been ordered to endea-vour to make our English youth care somewhat for the arts ; and must put my uttermost strength into that business.   To which end I must clear myself from all sense of responsibility for the material distress around me, by explaining to you, once for all, in the shortest English I can, what I know of its causes ; by pointing out to you some of the methods by which it might be relieved ; and by setting aside regularly some small percentage of my income, to assist, as one of yourselves, in what one and all we shall have to do ; each of us laying by something, according to our means, for the common service ; and having amongst us, at last, be it ever so small, a National Store instead of a National Debt.   Store which, once securely founded, will fast increase, provided only you take the pains to understand, and have perseverance to maintain, the elementary principles of Human Economy, which have, of late, not only been lost sight of, but wilfully and formally entombed under pyramids of falsehood.

And first I beg you most solemnly to convince yourselves of the partly comfortable, partly formidable fact, that your prosperity is in your own hands. That only in a remote degree does it depend on external matters, and least of all on forms of government. In all times of trouble the first thing to be done is to make the most of whatever forms of government you have got, by setting honest men to work them ; (the trouble, in all probability, having arisen only from the want of such ;) and for the rest, you must in no wise concern yourselves about them ; more particularly it would be lost time to do so at this moment, when whatever is popularly said about governments cannot but be absurd, for want of definition of terms. Consider, for instance, the ridiculousness of the division of parties into " Liberal " and " Conservative." There is no opposition whatever between those two kinds of men. There is opposition between Liberals and Illiberals ; that is to say, between people who desire liberty, and who dislike it. I am a violent Illiberal ; but it does not follow that I must be a Conservative. A Conservative is a person who wishes to keep things as they are ; and he is opposed to a Destructive, who wishes to destroy them, or to an Innovator, who wishes to alter them. Now, though I am an Illiberal, there are many things I should like to destroy. I should like to destroy most of the railroads in England, and all the railroads in Wales. I should like to destroy and rebuild the Houses of Parliament, the National Gallery, and the East end of London ; and to destroy, without rebuilding, the new town of Edinburgh, the north suburb of Geneva, and the city of New York. Thus in many things I am the reverse of Conservative ; nay, there are some long-established things which I hope to see changed before I die ; but I want still to keep the fields of England green, and her cheeks red ; and that girls should be taught to curtsey, and boys to take their hats off, when a Professor or otherwise dignified person passes by ; and that Kings should keep their crowns on their heads, and Bishops their crosiers in their hands; and should duly recognise the significance of the crown, and the use of the crook.

As you would find it thus impossible to class me justly in either party, so you would find it impossible to class any person whatever, who had clear and developed political opinions, and who could define them accurately. Men only associate in parties by sacrificing their opinions, or by having none worth sacrificing ; and the effect of party government is always to develope hostilities and hypocrisies, and to extinguish ideas.

Thus the so-called Monarchic and Republican parties have thrown Europe into conflagration and shame, merely for want of clear conception of the things they imagine themselves to fight for. The moment a Republic was proclaimed in France, Garibaldi came to fight for it as a " Holy Republic." But Garibaldi could not know,—no mortal creature could know,—whether it was going to be a Holy or Profane Republic. You cannot evoke any form of government by beat of drum. The proclamation of a government implies the considerate acceptance of a code of laws, and the appointment of means for their execution, neither of which things can be done in an instant. You may overthrow a government, and announce yourselves lawless, in the twinkling of an eye, as you can blow up a ship, or upset and sink one. But you can no more create a government with a word, than an ironclad.

No; nor can you even define its character in few words; the measure of sanctity in it depending on degrees of justice in the administration of law, which are often in-dependent of form altogether. Generally speaking, the community of thieves in London or Paris have adopted Republican Institutions, and live at this day without any acknowledged Captain or Head ; but under Robin Hood, brigandage in England, and under Sir John Hawkwood, brigandage in Italy, became strictly monarchical. Theft could not, merely by that dignified form of government, be made a holy manner of life ; but it was made both dexterous and decorous. The pages of the English knights under Sir John Hawkwood spent nearly all their spare time in burnishing the knight's armour, and made it always

so bright, that they were called "The White Company."
And the notary of Tortona, Azario, tells us of them, that
these foragers (*furatores*) "were more expert than any
plunderers in Lombardy. They for the most part sleep
by day, and watch by night, and have such plans and
artifices for taking towns, that never were the like or
equal of them witnessed."*

The actual Prussian expedition into France merely
differs from Sir John's in Italy by being more generally
savage, much less enjoyable, and by its clumsier devices
for taking towns ; for Sir John had no occasion to burn
their libraries. In neither case does the monarchical form
of government bestow any Divine right of theft ; but it
puts the available forces into a convenient form. Even with
respect to convenience only, it is not yet determinable
by the evidence of history, what is absolutely the best
form of government to live under. There are indeed
said to be republican villages (towns ?) in America, where
everybody is civil, honest, and substantially comfortable ;
but these villages have several unfair advantages—there are
no lawyers in them, no town councils, and no parliaments.
Such republicanism, if possible on a large scale, would be
worth fighting for ; though, in my own private mind, I
confess I should like to keep a few lawyers, for the sake of
their wigs, and the faces under them—generally very grand
when they are really good lawyers—and for their (unpro-

---

* Communicated to me by my friend Mr. Rawdon Brown, of Venice, from
his yet unpublished work, "The English in Italy in the 14th Century."

fessional) talk.   Also I should like to have a Parliament,
into which people might be elected on condition of their
never saying anything about politics, that one might still
feel sometimes that one was acquainted with an M.P.   In
the meantime Parliament is a luxury to the British squire,
and an honour to the British manufacturer, which you
may leave them to enjoy in their own way ; provided only
you make them always clearly explain, when they tax
you, what they want with your money ; and that you
understand yourselves, what money is, and how it is
got, and what it is good for, and bad for.

These matters I hope to explain to you in this and
some following letters ; which, among various other
reasons, it is necessary that I should write in order that
you may make no mistake as to the real economical results
of Art teaching, whether in the Universities or elsewhere.
I will begin by directing your attention particularly to
that point.

The first object of all work—not the principal one,
but the first and necessary one—is to get food, clothes,
lodging, and fuel.

It is quite possible to have too much of all these
things.   I know a great many gentlemen, who eat too
large dinners ; a great many ladies, who have too many
clothes.   I know there is lodging to spare in London, for
I have several houses there myself, which I can't let.
And I know there is fuel to spare everywhere, since we
get up steam to pound the roads with, while our men

stand idle ; or drink till they can't stand, idle, or any otherwise.

Notwithstanding, there is agonizing distress even in this highly favoured England, in some classes, for want of food, clothes, lodging, and fuel. And it has become a popular idea among the benevolent and ingenious, that you may in great part remedy these deficiencies by teaching, to these starving and shivering persons, Science and Art. In their way—as I do not doubt you will believe—I am very fond of both ; and I am sure it will be beneficial for the British nation to be lectured upon the merits of Michael Angelo, and the nodes of the moon. But I should strongly object my-self to being lectured on either, while I was hungry and cold ; and I suppose the same view of the matter would be taken by the greater number of British citizens in those predicaments. So that, I am con-vinced, their present eagerness for instruction in paint-ing and astronomy proceeds from an impression in their minds that, somehow, they may paint or star-gaze themselves into clothes and victuals. Now it is per-fectly true that you may sometimes sell a picture for a thousand pounds ; but the chances are greatly against your doing so—much more than the chances of a lottery. In the first place, you must paint a very clever picture ; and the chances are greatly against your doing that. In the second place, you must meet with an amiable picture-dealer ; and the chances are somewhat against your doing that. In the third place, the amiable picture-dealer must meet with a fool; and the chances are not always in favour even of his doing that—though, as I gave exactly the sum in question for a picture myself, only the other day, it is not for me to say so. Assume, however, to put the case most favourably, that what with the practical results of the energies of Mr. Cole, at Kensington, and the æsthetic impressions produced by various lectures at Cambridge and Oxford, the profits of art employment might be counted on as a rateable income. Suppose even that the ladies of the richer classes should come to delight no less in new pictures than in new dresses; and that picture-making should thus become as constant and lucrative an occupation as dress-making. Still, you know, they can't buy pictures and dresses too. If they buy two pictures a day, they can't buy two dresses a day; or if they do, they must save in something else. They have but a certain income, be it never so large. They spend that now; and you can't get more out of them. Even if they lay by money, the time comes when somebody must spend it. You will find that they do verily spend now all they have, neither more nor less. If ever they seem to spend more, it is only by running in debt, and not paying; if they for a time spend less, some day the overplus must come into circulation. All they have, they spend; more than that, they cannot at any time; less than that, they can only for a short time.

Whenever, therefore, any new industry, such as this of picture-making, is invented, of which the profits depend on patronage, it merely means that you have effected a diversion of the current of money in your own favour, and to somebody else's loss. Nothing, really, has been gained by the nation, though probably much time and wit, as well as sundry people's senses, have been lost. Before such a diversion can be effected, a great many kind things must have been done, a great deal of excellent advice given ; and an immense quantity of ingenious trouble taken : the arithmetical course of the business throughout being, that for every penny you are yourself better, somebody else is a penny the worse ; and the net result of the whole, precisely zero.

Zero, of course, I mean, so far as money is concerned. It may be more dignified for working women to paint than to embroider ; and it may be a very charming piece of self-denial, in a young lady, to order a high art fresco instead of a ball-dress ; but as far as cakes and ale are concerned, it is all the same,—there is but so much money to be got by you, or spent by her, and not one farthing more, usually a great deal less, by high art than by low. Zero, also, observe. I mean partly in a complimentary sense to the work executed. If you have done no good by painting, at least you have done no serious mischief. A bad picture is indeed a dull thing to have in a house, and in a certain sense

a mischievous thing ; but it won't blow the roof off.
Whereas, of most things which the English, French,
and Germans are paid for making now-a-days,—cart-
ridges, cannon, and the like,—you know the best thing
we can possibly hope is that they *may* be useless, and
the net result of them, zero.

The thing, therefore, that you have to ascertain
approximately, in order to determine on some consistent
organization, is the maximum of wages-fund you have
to depend on to start with, that is to say, virtually the
sum of the income of the gentleman of England. Do
not trouble yourselves at first about France or Germany,
or any other foreign country. The principle of free
trade is, that French gentlemen should employ English
workmen, for whatever the English can do better than
the French ; and that English gentlemen should employ
French workmen, for whatever the French can do better
than the English. It is a very right principle, but
merely extends the question to a wider field. Suppose,
for the present, that France, and every other country but
your own, were—what I suppose you would, if you had
your way, like them to be—sunk under water, and that
England were the only country in the world. Then, how
would you live in it most comfortably ? Find out that,
and you will then easily find how two countries can exist
together ; or more, not only without need for fighting, but
to each other's advantage.

For, indeed, the laws by which two next-door neighbours might live most happily—the one not being the better for his neighbour's poverty, but the worse, and the better for his neighbour's prosperity—are those also by which it is convenient and wise for two parishes, two provinces, or two kingdoms, to live side by side. And the nature of every commercial and military operation which takes place in Europe, or in the world, may always be best investigated by supposing it limited to the districts of a single country. Kent and Northumberland exchange hops and coals on precisely the same economical principles as Italy and England exchange oil for iron ; and the essential character of the war between Germany and France may be best understood by supposing it a dispute between Lancaster and Yorkshire for the line of the Ribble. Suppose that Lancashire, having absorbed Cumberland and Cheshire, and been much insulted and troubled by Yorkshire in consequence, and at last attacked ; and having victoriously repulsed the attack, and retaining old grudges against Yorkshire, about the colour of roses, from the fifteenth century, declares that it cannot possibly be safe against the attacks of Yorkshire any longer, unless it gets the townships of Giggleswick and Wigglesworth, and a fortress on Pen-y-gent. Yorkshire replying that this is totally inadmissible, and that it will eat its last horse, and perish to its last Yorkshireman, rather than part with a stone of Giggleswick, a crag of Pen-y-gent, or a ripple of Ribble,— Lancashire with its Cumbrian and Cheshire contingents

invades Yorkshire, and meeting with much Divine assistance, ravages the West Riding, and besieges York on
Christmas day. That is the actual gist of the whole
business ; and in the same manner you may see the
downright common sense—if any is to be seen—of other
human proceedings, by taking them first under narrow
and homely conditions. So, for the present, we will
fancy ourselves, what you tell me you all want to be,
independent: we will take no account of any other country
but Britain ; and on that condition I will begin to show
you in my next paper how we ought to live, after ascer-
taining the utmost limits of the wages-fund, which means
the income of our gentlemen ; that is to say, essentially,
the income of those who have command of the land, and
therefore of all food.

What you call " wages," practically, is the quantity
of food which the possessor of the land gives you, to
work for him. There is, finally, no " capital " but that.
If all the money of all the capitalists in the whole world
were destroyed, the notes and bills burnt, the gold
irrecoverably buried, and all the machines and apparatus
of manufactures crushed, by a mistake in signals, in one
catastrophe ; and nothing remained but the land, with its
animals and vegetables, and buildings for shelter,—the
poorer population would be very little worse off than
they are at this instant ; and their labour, instead of
being " limited " by the destruction, would be greatly
stimulated. They would feed themselves from the ani-

mals and growing crops ; heap here and there a few tons of ironstone together, build rough walls round them to get a blast, and in a fortnight, they would have iron tools again, and be ploughing and fighting, just as usual. It is only we who had the capital who would suffer ; we should not be able to live idle, as we do now, and many of us—I, for instance—should starve at once : but you, though little the worse, would none of you be the better eventually, for our loss—or starvation. The removal of superfluous mouths would indeed benefit you somewhat, for a time ; but you would soon replace them with hungrier ones ; and there are many of us who are quite worth our meat to you in different ways, which I will explain in due place : also I will show you that our money is really likely to be useful to you in its accumulated form, (besides that, in the instances when it has been won by work, it justly belongs to us,) so only that you are careful never to let us persuade you into borrowing it, and paying us interest for it. You will find a very amusing story, explaining your position in that case, at the 117th page of the ' Manual of Political Economy,' published this year at Cambridge, for your early instruction, in an almost devotionally catechetical form, by Messrs. Macmillan.

Perhaps I had better quote it to you entire : it is taken by the author " from the French."

There was once in a village a poor carpenter, who worked hard from morning to night. One day James thought to himself,

" With my hatchet, saw, and hammer, I can only make coarse furniture, and can only get the pay for such. If I had a plane, I should please my customers more, and they would pay me more. Yes, I am resolved, I will make myself a plane." At the end of ten days, James had in his possession an admirable plane which he valued all the more for having made it himself. Whilst he was reckoning all the profits which he expected to derive from the use of it, he was interrupted by William, a carpenter in the neighbouring village. William, having admired the plane, was struck with the advantages which might be gained from it. He said to James—

" You must do me a service; lend me the plane for a year." As might be expected, James cried out, " How can you think of such a thing, William? Well, if I do you this service, what will you do for me in return? "

W. Nothing. Don't you know that a loan ought to be gratuitous?

J. I know nothing of the sort; but I do know that if I were to lend you my plane for a year, it would be giving it to you. To tell you the truth, that was not what I made it for.

W. Very well, then; I ask you to do me a service; what service do you ask me in return?

J. First, then, in a year the plane will be done for. You must therefore give me another exactly like it.

W. That is perfectly just. I submit to these conditions. I think you must be satisfied with this, and can require nothing further.

J. I think otherwise. I made the plane for myself, and not for you. I expected to gain some advantage from it. I have made the plane for the purpose of improving my work and my condition; if you merely return it to me in a year, it is you who will gain the profit of it during the whole of that time. I am not bound to do you such a service without receiving anything in return. Therefore, if you wish for my plane, besides the restoration already bargained for, you must give me a new plank as a compensation for the advantages of which I shall be deprived.

These terms were agreed to, but the singular part of it is that at the end of the year, when the plane came into James's possession, he lent it again; recovered it, and lent it a third and fourth time. It has passed into the hands of his son, who still lends it. Let us examine this little story. The plane is the symbol of all capital, and the plank is the symbol of all interest.

If this be an abridgment, what a graceful piece of highly wrought literature the original story must be! I take the liberty of abridging it a little more.

James makes a plane, lends it to William on 1st January for a year. William gives him a plank for the loan of it, wears it out, and makes another for James, which he gives him on 31st December. On 1st January he again borrows the new one; and the arrangement is repeated continuously. The position of William therefore is, that he makes a plane every 31st of December; lends it to James till the next day, and pays James a plank annually for the privilege of lending it to him on that evening. This, in future investigations of capital and interest, we will call, if you please, "the Position of William."

You may not at the first glance see where the fallacy lies (the writer of the story evidently counts on your not seeing it at all).

If James did not lend the plane to William, he could

only get his gain of a plank by working with it himself, and wearing it out himself. When he had worn it
out at the end of the year, he would, therefore, have
to make another for himself. William, working with
it instead, gets the advantage instead, which he must,
therefore, pay James his plank for ; and return to James,
what James would, if he had not lent his plane, then
have had—not a new plane—but the worn-out one,
James must make a new one for himself, as he would
have had to do if no William had existed ; and if
William likes to borrow it again for another plank—
all is fair.

That is to say, clearing the story of its nonsense,
that James makes a plane annually, and sells it to
William for its proper price, which, in kind, is a new
plank. But this arrangement has nothing whatever to
do with principal or with interest. There are, indeed,
many very subtle conditions involved in any sale ; one
among which is the value of ideas ; I will explain that
value to you in the course of time ; (the article is not
one which modern political economists have any fami-
liarity with dealings in ;) and I will tell you somewhat
also of the real nature of interest ; but if you will only
get, for the present, a quite clear idea of " the Position
of William," it is all I want of you.

I remain, your faithful friend,

JOHN RUSKIN.

FORS CLAVIGERA.

LETTER THE 2nd.

THE GREAT PICNIC.

DENMARK HILL,
1st February, 1871.

FRIENDS,——

Before going farther, you may like to know, and ought to know, what I mean by the title of these Letters ; and why it is in Latin. I can only tell you in part, for the Letters will be on many things, if I am able to carry out my plan in them ; and that title means many things, and is in Latin, because I could not have given an English one that meant so many. We, indeed, were not till lately a loquacious people, nor a useless one ; but the Romans did more, and said less, than any other nation that ever lived ; and their language is the most heroic ever spoken by men.

Therefore I wish you to know, at least, some words of it, and to recognise what thoughts they stand for.

Some day, I hope you may know—and that European workmen may know—many words of it ; but even a few will be useful.

II.]

Do not smile at my saying so. Of Arithmetic, Geo-
metry, and Chemistry, you can know but little, at the
utmost ; but that little, well learnt, serves you well. And
a little Latin, well learnt, will serve you also, and in a
higher way than any of these.

'Fors' is the best part of three good English words,
Force, Fortitude, and Fortune. I wish you to know the
meaning of those three words accurately.

'Force' (in humanity), means power of doing good
work. A fool, or a corpse, can do any quantity of mischief; but only a wise and strong man, or, with what
true vital force there is in him, a weak one, can do
good.

'Fortitude' means the power of bearing necessary
pain, or trial of patience, whether by time, or temptation.

'Fortune' means the necessary fate of a man : the
ordinance of his life which cannot be changed. To
'make your Fortune' is to rule that appointed fate to
the best ends of which it is capable.

Fors is a feminine word ; and Clavigera, is, therefore,
the feminine of 'Claviger.'

Clava means a club. Clavis, a key. Clavus, a nail, or
a rudder.

Gero means 'I carry.' It is the root of our word
'gesture' (the way you carry yourself) ; and, in a curious
bye-way, of 'jest.'

Clavigera may mean, therefore, either Club-bearer,
Key-bearer, or Nail-bearer.

Each of these three possible meanings of Clavigera corresponds to one of the three meanings of Fors.

Fors, the Club-bearer, means the strength of Hercules, or of Deed.

Fors, the Key-bearer, means the strength of Ulysses, or of Patience.

Fors, the Nail-bearer, means the strength of Lycurgus, or of Law.

I will tell you what you may usefully know of those three Greek persons in a little time. At present, note only of the three powers: 1. That the strength of Hercules is for deed, not misdeed; and that his club—the favourite weapon, also, of the Athenian hero Theseus, whose form is the best inheritance left to us by the greatest of Greek sculptors, (it is in the Elgin room of the British Museum, and I shall have much to tell you of him—especially how he helped Hercules in his utmost need, and how he invented mixed vegetable soup)—was for subduing monsters and cruel persons, and was of olive-wood. 2. That the Second Fors Clavigera is portress at a gate which she cannot open till you have waited long; and that her robe is of the colour of ashes, or dry earth.* 3. That the third Fors Clavigera, the power of Lycurgus, is Royal as well as Legal; and that the notablest crown yet existing in Europe of any that have been worn by Christian kings, was—people say—made of a Nail.

* See Carey's translation of the ninth book of Dante's 'Purgatory,'

That is enough about my title, for this time ; now to our work. I told you, and you will find it true, that, practically all wages mean the food and lodging given you by the possessors of the land.

It begins to be asked on many sides how the possessors of the land became possessed of it, and why they should still possess it, more than you or I ; and Ricardo's 'Theory' of Rent, though, for an economist, a very creditably ingenious work of fiction, will not much longer be imagined to explain the 'Practice' of Rent.

The true answer, in this matter, as in all others, is the best. Some land has been bought ; some, won by cultivation : but the greater part, in Europe, seized originally by force of hand.

You may think, in that case, you would be justified in trying to seize some yourselves, in the same way.

If you could, you, and your children, would only hold it by the same title as its present holders. If it is a bad one, you had better not so hold it ; if a good one, you had better let the present holders alone.

And in any case, it is expedient that you should do so, for the present holders, whom we may generally call 'Squires' (a title having three meanings, like Fors, and all good ; namely, Rider, Shield-bearer, and Carver), are quite the best men you can now look to for leading : it is too true that they have much demoralized themselves lately by horse-racing, bird-shooting, and vermin-hunting ;

and most of all by living in London, instead of on their
estates ; but they are still (without exception) brave ;
nearly without exception, good-natured ; honest, so far
as they understand honesty ; and much to be depended
on, if once you and they understand each other.

Which you are far enough now from doing ; and it is
imminently needful that you should : so we will have an
accurate talk of them soon. The needfullest thing of all
first is that you should know the functions of the persons
whom you are being taught to think of as your protectors
against the Squires ;—your ' Employers,' namely ; or
Capitalist Supporters of Labour.

' Employers.' It is a noble title. If, indeed, they have
found you idle, and given you employment, wisely,—let
us no more call them mere ' Men ' of Business, but rather
' Angels ' of Business : quite the best sort of Guardian
Angel.

Yet are you sure it is necessary, absolutely, to look to
superior natures for employment ? Is it inconceivable
that you should employ—yourselves ? I ask the question,
because these Seraphic beings, undertaking also to be
Seraphic Teachers or Doctors, have theories about
employment which may perhaps be true in their own
celestial regions, but are inapplicable under worldly conditions.

To one of these principles, announced by themselves
as highly important, I must call your attention closely,
because it has of late been the cause of much embar-

rassment among persons in a sub-seraphic life. I take its statement verbatim, from the 25th page of the Cambridge catechism before quoted :

"This brings us to a most important proposition respecting capital, one which it is essential that the student should thoroughly understand.

"The proposition is this—A demand for commodities is not a demand for labour.

"The demand for labour depends upon the amount of capital : the demand for commodities simply determines in what direction labour shall be employed.

"AN EXAMPLE.—The truth of these assertions can best be shown by examples. Let us suppose that a manufacturer of woollen cloth is in the habit of spending £50 annually in lace. What does it matter, say some, whether he spends this £50 in lace or whether he uses it to employ more labourers in his own business ? Does not the £50 spent in lace maintain the labourers who make the lace, just the same as it would maintain the labourers who make cloth, if the manufacturer used the money in extending his own business ? If he ceased buying the lace, for the sake of employing more cloth-makers, would there not be simply a transfer of the £50 from the lace-makers to the cloth-makers ? In order to find the right answer to these questions, let us imagine what would actually take place if the manufacturer ceased buying the lace, and employed the £50 in paying the wages of an additional number of cloth-makers. The lace manufacturer, in consequence of the diminished demand for lace, would diminish the production, and would withdraw from his business an amount of capital corresponding to the diminished demand. As there is no reason to suppose that the lace-maker would, on losing some of his custom, become more extravagant, or would cease to desire to derive income from the capital which the diminished demand has caused him to withdraw from his own business, it may be assumed that he would invest this capital in some other industry. This capital is not the same as that which his former customer, the woollen cloth manufacturer, is now paying his own labourers with ; it is a second capital ; and in the place of £50 employed in maintaining labour, there is now £100 so employed. There is no transfer from lace-makers to cloth-makers. There is fresh employment for the cloth-makers, and a transfer from the lace-makers to some other labourers."—*Principles of Political Economy*, vol. i., p. 102.

This is very fine ; and it is clear that we may carry forward the improvement in our commercial arrangements by recommending all the other customers of the lace-maker to treat him as the cloth-maker has done. Whereupon he of course leaves the lace business entirely, and uses all his capital in ' some other industry.' Having thus established the lace-maker with a complete ' second capital,' in the other industry, we will next proceed to develope a capital out of the cloth-maker, by recommending all *his* customers to leave *him.* Whereupon, he will also invest his capital in ' some other industry,' and we have a Third capital, employed in the National benefit.

We will now proceed in the round of all possible businesses, developing a correspondent number of new capitals, till we come back to our friend the lace-maker again, and find him employed in whatever his new industry was. By now taking away again all his new customers, we begin the development of another order of Capitals in a higher Seraphic circle—and so develope at last an Infinite Capital !

It would be difficult to match this for simplicity ; it is more comic even than the fable of James and William, though you may find it less easy to detect the fallacy here ; but the obscurity is not because the error is less gross, but because it is threefold. Fallacy 1st is the assumption that a cloth-maker may employ any number of men, whether he has customers or not ; while a lace-maker must dismiss his men if he has not customers. Fallacy 2nd : That when a lace-maker can no longer find customers for lace, he can always find customers for something else. Fallacy 3rd (the essential one) : That the funds provided by these new customers, produced seraphically from the clouds, are a 'second capital.' Those customers, if they exist now, existed before the lace-maker adopted his new business ; and were the employers of the people in that business. If the lace-maker gets them, he merely diverts their fifty pounds from the tradesman they were before employing, to himself; and that is Mr. Mill's 'second capital.'

Underlying these three fallacies, however, there is, in the mind of 'the greatest thinker in England,' some consciousness of a partial truth, which he has never yet been able to define for himself—still less to explain to others. The real root of them is his conviction that it is beneficial and profitable to make broadcloth ; and

unbeneficial and unprofitable to make lace ;* so that the
trade of cloth-making should be infinitely extended, and
that of lace-making infinitely repressed. Which is, indeed, partially true. Making cloth, if it be well made,
is a good industry; and if you had sense enough to
read your Walter Scott thoroughly, I should invite you
to join me in sincere hope that Glasgow might in that
industry long flourish ; and the chief hostelry at Aberfoil
be at the sign of the " Nicol Jarvie." Also, of lace-
makers, it is often true that they had better be doing
something else. I admit it, with no good will, for I
know a most kind lady, a clergyman's wife, who devotes
her life to the benefit of her country by employing lace-
makers; and all her friends make presents of collars and
cuffs to each other, for the sake of charity; and as, if
they did not, the poor girl lace-makers would probably
indeed be 'diverted' into some other less diverting
industry, in due assertion of the rights of women,
(cartridge-filling, or percussion-cap making, most likely,)
I even go the length, sometimes, of furnishing my friend
with a pattern, and never say a word to disturb her
young customers in their conviction that it is an act of
Christian charity to be married in more than ordinarily
expensive veils.

But there *is* one kind of lace for which I should be

* I assume the Cambridge quotation to be correct : in my old edition
(1848), the distinction is between 'weavers and lace-makers' and 'journeymen
bricklayers ; ' and making velvet is considered to be the production of
a 'commodity,' but building a house only doing a 'service.'

glad that the demand ceased. Iron lace. If we must even doubt whether ornamental thread-work may be, wisely, made on cushions in the sunshine, by dexterous fingers for fair shoulders,—how are we to think of Ornamental Iron-work, made with deadly sweat of men, and steady waste, all summer through, of the coals that Earth gave us for winter fuel? What shall we say of labour spent on lace such as that?

Nay, says the Cambridge catechism, "the demand for commodities is not a demand for labour."

Doubtless, in the economist's new earth, cast iron will be had for asking: the hapless and brave Parisians find it even rain occasionally out of the new economical Heavens, *without* asking. Gold will also one day, perhaps, be begotten of gold, until the supply of that, as well as of iron, may be, at least, equal to the demand. But, in this world, it is not so yet. Neither thread-lace, gold-lace, iron-lace, nor stone-lace, whether they be commodities or incommodities, can be had for nothing. How much, think you, did the gilded flourishes cost round the gas-lamps on Westminster Bridge? or the stone-lace of the pinnacles of the temple of Parliament at the end of it, (incommodious enough, as I hear;) or the point-lace of the park-railings which you so improperly pulled down, when you wanted to be Parliamentary yourselves; (much good you would have got of that l) or the 'openwork' of iron railings generally—the special glories of English design? Will you count the cost, in labour and coals, of the

blank bars ranged along all the melancholy miles of our
suburban streets, saying with their rusty tongues, as plainly
as iron tongues can speak, " Thieves outside, and nothing
to steal within " ?   A beautiful wealth they are! and a
productive capital !   " Well, but," you answer, " the making
them was work for us."   Of course it was ; is not that the
very thing I am telling you ?   Work it was ; and too much.
But will you be good enough to make up your minds,
once for all, whether it is really work that you want, or
rest ?   I thought you rather objected to your quantity of
work ;—that you were all for having eight hours of it
instead of ten ? You may have twelve instead of ten, easily,
—sixteen, if you like ! If it is only occupation you want,
why do you cast the iron ? Forge it in the fresh air, on
a workman's anvil ; make iron-lace like this of Verona,—

every link of it swinging loose like a knight's chain mail : then you may have some joy of it afterwards, and pride ; and say you knew the cunning of a man's right hand. But I think it is pay that you want, not work ; and it is very true that pretty iron-work like that does not pay ; but it *is* pretty, and it might even be entertaining, if you made those leaves at the top of it (which are, as far as I can see, only artichoke, and not very well done) in the likeness of all the beautiful leaves you could find, till you knew them all by heart. " Wasted time and hammer-strokes," say you ? " A wise people like the English will have nothing but spikes ; and, besides, the spikes are highly needful, so many of the wise people being thieves." Yes, that is so ; and, therefore, in calculating the annual cost of keeping your thieves, you must always reckon, not only the cost of the spikes that keep them in, but of the spikes that keep them out. But how if, instead of flat rough spikes, you put triangular polished ones, commonly called bayonets ; and instead of the perpendicular bars, put perpendicular men ? What is the cost to you then, of your railing, of which you must feed the idle bars daily ? Costly enough, if it stays quiet. But how, if it begin to march and countermarch ? and apply its spikes horizontally ?

And now note this that follows ; it is of vital importance to you.

There are, practically, two absolutely opposite kinds of labour going on among men, for ever.*

The first, labour supported by Capital, producing nothing.

The second, labour unsupported by Capital, producing all things.

Take two simple and precise instances on a small scale.

A little while since, I was paying a visit in Ireland, and chanced to hear an account of the pleasures of a picnic party, who had gone to see a waterfall. There was of course ample lunch, feasting on the grass, and basketsful of fragments taken up afterwards.

Then the company, feeling themselves dull, gave the fragments that remained to the attendant ragged boys, on condition that they should ' pull each other's hair.'

Here, you see, is, in the most accurate sense, employment of food, or capital, in the support of entirely unproductive labour.

Next, for the second kind. I live at the top of a short but rather steep hill ; at the bottom of which, every day, all the year round, but especially in frost, coal-waggons

---

* I do not mean that there are no other kinds, nor that well-paid labour must necessarily be unproductive. I hope to see much done, some day, for just pay, and wholly productive. But these, named in the text, are the two opposite extremes ; and, in actual life, hitherto, the largest means have been usually spent in mischief, and the most useful work done for the worst pay.

get stranded, being economically provided with the smallest number of horses that can get them along on level ground.

The other day, when the road, frozen after thaw, was at the worst, my assistant, the engraver of that bit of iron-work on the 11th page, was coming up here, and found three coal-waggons at a lock, helpless ; the drivers, as usual, explaining Political Economy to the horses, by beating them over the heads.

There were half a dozen fellows besides, out of work, or not caring to be in it—standing by, looking on. My engraver put his shoulder to a wheel, (at least his hand to a spoke,) and called on the idlers to do as much. They didn't seem to have thought of such a thing, but were ready enough when called on. " And we went up screaming," said Mr. Burgess.

Do you suppose that was one whit less proper human work than going up a hill against a battery, merely because, in that case, half of the men would have gone down, screaming, instead of up ; and those who got up would have done no good at the top ?

But observe the two opposite kinds of labour. The first lavishly supported by Capital, and producing Nothing. The second, unsupported by any Capital whatsoever,— not having so much as a stick for a tool,—but called, by mere goodwill, out of the vast void of the world's Idle- ness, and producing the definitely profitable result of moving a weight of fuel some distance towards the place where it was wanted, and sparing the strength of over-loaded creatures.

Observe further. The labour producing no useful result was demoralizing. All such labour is.

The labour producing useful result was educational in its influence on the temper. All such labour is.

And the first condition of education, the thing you are all crying out for, is being put to wholesome and useful work. And it is nearly the last conditions of it, too ; you need very little more ; but, as things go, there will yet be difficulty in getting that. As things have hitherto gone, the difficulty has been to avoid getting the reverse of that.

For, during the last eight hundred years, the upper classes of Europe have been one large Picnic Party. Most of them have been religious also ; and in sitting down, by companies, upon the green grass, in parks, gardens, and the like, have considered themselves com-manded into that position by Divine authority, and fed with bread from Heaven : of which they duly considered it proper to bestow the fragments in support, and the tithes in tuition, of the poor.

But, without even such small cost, they might have taught the poor many beneficial things. In some places they *have* taught them manners, which is already much. They might have cheaply taught them merriment also :— dancing and singing, for instance. The young English ladies who sit nightly to be instructed, themselves, at

some cost, in melodies illustrative of the consumption
of La Traviata, and the damnation of Don Juan, might
have taught every girl peasant in England to join in
costless choirs of innocent song.   Here and there, perhaps, a gentleman might have been found able to teach
his peasantry some science and art.   Science and fine
art don't pay ; but they cost little.   Tithes—not of the
income of the country, but of the income, say, of its
brewers—nay, probably the sum devoted annually by
England to provide drugs for the adulteration of its own
beer,—would have founded lovely little museums, and
perfect libraries, in every village.   And if here and there
an English churchman had been found (such as Dean
Stanley) willing to explain to peasants the sculpture of
his and their own cathedral, and to read its black-letter
inscriptions for them ; and, on warm Sundays, when they
were too sleepy to attend to anything more proper—to
tell them a story about some of the people who had
built it, or lay buried in it—we perhaps might have been
quite as religious as we are, and yet need not now have
been offering prizes for competition in art schools, nor
lecturing with tender sentiment on the inimitableness of
the works of Fra Angelico.

These things the great Picnic Party might have taught
without cost, and with amusement to themselves.   One
thing, at least, they were bound to teach, whether it
amused them or not ;—how, day by day, the daily bread
they expected their village children to pray to God for,

might be earned in accordance with the laws of God. *This* they might have taught, not only without cost, but with great gain.   One thing only they *have* taught, and at considerable cost.

They have spent four hundred millions* of pounds here in England within the last twenty years !—how much in France and Germany, I will take some pains to ascertain for you,—and with this initial outlay of capital, have taught the peasants of Europe—to pull each other's hair.

With *this* result, 17th January, 1871, at and around the chief palace of their own pleasures, and the chief city of their delights :

" Each demolished house has its own legend of sorrow, of pain, and horror ; each vacant doorway speaks to the eye, and almost to the ear, of hasty flight, as armies or fire came—of weeping women and trembling children running away in awful fear, abandoning the home that saw their birth, the old house they loved— of startled men seizing quickly under each arm their most valued goods, and rushing, heavily laden, after their wives and babes, leaving to hostile hands the task of burning all the rest.   When evening falls, the wretched outcasts, worn with fatigue and tears, reach Versailles, St. Germain, or some other place outside the range of fire, and there they beg for bread and shelter, homeless, foodless, broken with despair.   And this, remember, has been the

---

* £992,740,328, in seventeen years, say the working men of Burnley, in their address just issued—an excellent address in its way, and full of very fair arithmetic—if its facts are all right ; only I don't see, myself, how, " from fifteen to twenty-five millions per annum," make nine hundred and ninety-two millions in seventeen years.

fate of something like a hundred thousand people during the last four months. Versailles alone has about fifteen thousand such fugitives to keep alive, all ruined, all hopeless, all vaguely asking the grim future what still worse fate it may have in store for them."—*Daily Telegraph*, Jan. 17th, 1871.

This is the result round their pleasant city, and *this* within their industrious and practical one : let us keep, for the reference of future ages, a picture of domestic life, out of the streets of London in her commercial prosperity, founded on the eternal laws of Supply and Demand, as applied by the modern Capitalist:

"A father in the last stage of consumption—two daughters nearly marriageable with hardly sufficient rotting clothing to 'cover their shame.' The rags that hang around their attenuated frames flutter in strips against their naked legs. They have no stool or chair upon which they can sit. Their father occupies the only stool in the room. They have no employment by which they can earn even a pittance. They are at home starving on a half-chance meal a day, and hiding their raggedness from the world. The walls are bare, there is one bed in the room, and a bundle of dirty rags are upon it. The dying father will shortly follow the dead mother ; and when the parish coffin encloses his wasted form, and a pauper's grave closes above him, what shall be his daughters' lot? This is but a type of many other homes in the district : dirt, misery, and disease alone flourish in that wretched neighbourhood. 'Fever and smallpox rage,' as the inhabitants say, 'next door, and next door, and over the way, and next door to that, and further down.' The living, dying, and dead are all huddled together. The houses have no ventilation, the back yards are receptacles for all sorts of filth and rubbish, the old barrels or vessels that contain the supply of water are thickly coated on the sides with slime, and there is an undisturbed deposit of mud at the bottom. There is no mortuary house—the dead lie in the dogholes where they breathed their last, and add to the contagion which spreads through the neighbourhood."— *Pall Mall Gazette*, January 7th, 1871, quoting the *Builder.*

As I was revising this sheet,—on the evening of the 20th of last month,—two slips of paper were brought to me. One contained, in consecutive paragraphs, an extract from the speech of one of the best and kindest of our public men, to the 'Liberal Association' at Portsmouth ; and an account of the performances of the 35-ton gun called the 'Woolwich infant' which is fed with 700-pound shot, and 130 pounds of gunpowder at one mouthful ; not at all like the Wapping infants, starving on a half-chance meal a day. "The gun was fired with the most satisfactory result," nobody being hurt, and nothing damaged but the platform, while the shot passed through the screens in front at the rate of 1,303 feet per second: and it seems, also, that the Woolwich infant has not seen the light too soon. For Mr. Cowper-Temple, in the preceding paragraph, informs the Liberals of Portsmouth, that in consequence of our amiable neutrality "we must contemplate the contingency of a combined fleet coming from the ports of, Prussia, Russia, and America, and making an attack on England."

Contemplating myself these relations of Russia, Prussia, Woolwich, and Wapping, it seems to my uncommercial mind merely like another case of iron railings—thieves outside, and nothing to steal within. But the second slip of paper announced approaching help in a peaceful direction. It was the prospectus of the Board-men's and General Advertising Co-operative Society, which invites, from the "generosity of the public, a necessary small preliminary sum," and, "in addition to the above, a small sum of money by way of capital," to set the members of the society up in the profitable business of walking about London between two boards. Here *is* at last found for us, then, it appears, a line of life! At the West End, lounging about the streets, with a well-made back to one's coat, and front to one's shirt, is usually thought of as not much in the way of business; but, doubtless, to lounge at the East End about the streets, with one Lie pinned to the front of you, and another to the back of you, will pay, in time, only with proper preliminary expenditure of capital. My friends, I repeat my question : Do you not think you could con-trive some little method of employing—yourselves? for truly I think the Seraphic Doctors are nearly at their wits' end (if ever their wits had a beginning). Tradesmen are beginning to find it difficult to live by lies of their own ; and workmen will not find it much easier to live, by walking about, flattened between other people's.

Think over it. On the first of March, I hope to ask you to read a little history with me; perhaps also, because the world's time, seen truly, is but one long and fitful April, in which every day is All Fools' day,—we may continue our studies in that month ; but on the first of May, you shall consider with me what you can do, or let me, if still living, tell you what I know you can do—those of you, at least, who will promise— (with the help of the three strong Fates), these three things :

1. To do your own work well, whether it be for life or death.

2. To help other people at theirs, when you can, and seek to avenge no injury.

3. To be sure you can obey good laws before you seek to alter bad ones.

Believe me,

Your faithful friend,

JOHN RUSKIN.

FORS CLAVIGERA.

LETTER THE 3rd.

RICHARD OF ENGLAND.

DENMARK HILL,
1st March, 1871.

MY FRIENDS,

We are to read—with your leave—some history to-day; the leave, however, will perhaps not willingly be given, for you may think that of the late you have read enough history, or too much, in *Gazettes* of morning and evening. No; you have read, and can read, no history in these. Reports of daily events, yes;—and if any journal would limit itself to statements of well-sifted fact, making itself not a " news "paper, but an " olds "paper, and giving its statements tested and true, like old wine, as soon as things could be known accurately; choosing also, of the many things that might be known, those which it was most vital to know, and summing them in few words of pure English,—I cannot say whether it would ever pay well to sell it; but I am sure it would pay well to read it, and to read no other.

But even so, to know only what was happening day by

day, would not be to read history. What happens now is but the momentary scene of a great play, of which you can understand nothing without some knowledge of the former action. And of that, so great a play is it, you can at best understand little ; yet of history, as of science, a little, well known, will serve you much, and a little, ill known, will do you fatally the contrary of service.

For instance, all your journals will be full of talk, for months to come, about whose fault the war was ; and you yourselves, as you begin to feel its deadly recoil on your own interests, or as you comprehend better the misery it has brought on others, will be looking about more and more restlessly for some one to accuse of it. That is because you don't know the law of Fate, nor the course of history. It is the law of Fate that we shall live, in part, by our own efforts, but in the greater part, by the help of others ; and that we shall also die, in part, for our own faults ; but in the greater part for the faults of others. Do you suppose (to take the thing on the small scale in which you can test it) that those seven children torn into pieces out of their sleep, in the last night of the siege of Paris,* had sinned above all the children in Paris, or above yours ? or that their parents had sinned more than you ? Do you think the thousands of soldiers, German and French, who have died in agony, and of women who have died of grief, had sinned above all other soldiers, or mothers, or girls, there and here ?

* *Daily Telegraph,* 30th January, 1871.

It was not their fault, but their Fate. The thing appointed to them by the Third Fors. But you think it was at least the Emperor Napoleon's fault, if not theirs? Or Count Bismarck's? No; not at all. The Emperor Napoleon had no more to do with it than a cork on the top of a wave has with the toss of the sea. Count Bismarck had very little to do with it. When the Count sent for my waiter, last July, in the village of Lauterbrunnen, among the Alps,—that the waiter then and there packed his knapsack and departed, to be shot, if need were, leaving my dinner unserved (as has been the case with many other people's dinners since)—depended on things much anterior to Count Bismarck. The two men who had most to answer for in the mischief of the matter were St. Louis and his brother, who lived in the middle of the thirteenth century. One, among the very best of men; and the other, of all that I ever read of, the worst. The good man, living in mistaken effort, and dying miserably, to the ruin of his country; the bad man living in triumphant good fortune, and dying peaceably, to the ruin of many countries. Such were their Fates, and ours. I am not going to tell you of them, nor anything about the French war to-day; and you have been told, long ago, (only you would not listen, nor believe,) the root of the modern German power—in that rough father of Frederick, who "yearly made his country richer, and this not in money alone (which is of very uncertain value, and sometimes has no value at all, and even less), but in frugality, diligence, punctuality, veracity,—the grand fountains from which money, and all real *values* and valours, spring for men. As a Nation's *Husband*, he seeks his fellow among Kings, ancient and modern. Happy the nation which gets such a Husband, once in the half thousand years. The Nation, as foolish wives and Nations do, repines and grudges a good deal, its weak whims and will being thwarted very often ; but it advances steadily, with consciousness or not, in the way of well-doing ; and, after long times, the harvest of this diligent sowing becomes manifest to the Nation, and to all Nations."*

No such harvest is sowing for you,—Freemen and Independent Electors of Parliamentary representatives, as you think yourselves.

Freemen, indeed ! You are slaves, not to masters of any strength or honour ; but to the idlest talkers at that floral end of Westminster bridge. Nay, to countless meaner masters than they. For though, indeed, as early as the year 1102, it was decreed in a council at St. Peter's, Westminster, "that no man for the future should presume to carry on the wicked trade of selling men in the markets, like brute beasts, which hitherto hath been the common custom of England," the no less wicked trade of *under-selling* men in markets has lasted to this day ; producing conditions of slavery differing from the ancient ones only in being starved instead of full-fed : and besides this, a

* Carlyle's *Frederick*, Book IV., chap. iii.

state of slavery unheard of among the nations till now,
has arisen with us. In all former slaveries, Egyptian,
Algerine, Saxon, and American, the slave's complaint
has been of compulsory *work*. But the modern Politico-
Economic slave is a new and far more injured species,
condemned to Compulsory *Idleness*, for fear he should
spoil other people's trade ; the beautifully logical condition of the national Theory of Economy in this matter
being that, if you are a shoemaker, it is a law of Heaven
that you must sell your goods under their price, in order
to destroy the trade of other shoemakers ; but if you
are not a shoemaker, and are going shoeless and lame,
it is a law of Heaven that you must not cut yourself a
bit of cowhide, to put between your foot and the stones,
because that would interfere with the total trade of
shoemaking.

Which theory, of all the wonderful— !

* * * *.

We will wait till April to consider of it ; meantime,
here is a note I have received from Mr. Alsager A. Hill,
who having been unfortunately active in organizing that
new effort in the advertising business, designed, as it seems,
on this loveliest principle of doing nothing that will be
perilously productive—was hurt by my manner of mention
of it in the last number of *Fors*. I offered accordingly to
print any form of remonstrance he would furnish me with,
if laconic enough ; and he writes to me, " The intention
of the Boardmen's Society is not, as the writer of *Fors*

Clavigera suggests, to ' find a line of life ' for able-bodied labourers, but simply, by means of co-operation, to give them the fullest benefit of their labour whilst they continue a very humble but still remunerative calling. See Rule 12. The capital asked for to start the organization is essential in all industrial partnerships, and in so poor a class of labour as that of street board-carrying could not be supplied by the men themselves. With respect to the ' lies ' alleged to be carried in front and behind, it is rather hard measure to say that mere announcements of public meetings or places of entertainments (of which street notices chiefly consist) are necessarily falsehoods."

To which, I have only to reply that I never said the newly-found line of life was meant for able-bodied persons. The distinction between able and unable-bodied men is entirely indefinite. There are all degrees of ability for all things ; and a man who can do anything, however little, should be made to do that little usefully. If you can carry about a board with a bill on it, you can carry, not about, but where it is wanted, a board *without* a bill on it ; which is a much more useful exercise of your ability. Respecting the general probity, and historical or descriptive accuracy, of advertisements, and their function in modern economy, I will inquire in another place. You see I use none for this book, and shall in future use none for any of my books ; having grave objection even to the very small minority of advertisements which are approximately true. I am correcting this sheet in the "Crown and Thistle" inn at Abingdon, and under my window is a shrill-voiced person, slowly progressive, crying, "Soles, three pair for a shillin'." In a market regulated by reason and order, instead of demand and supply, the soles would neither have been kept long enough to render such advertisement of them necessary, nor permitted, after their inexpedient preservation, to be advertised.

Of all attainable liberties, then, be sure first to strive for leave to be useful. Independence you had better cease to talk of, for you are dependent not only on every act of people whom you never heard of, who are living round you, but on every past act of what has been dust for a thousand years. So also, does the course of a thousand years to come, depend upon the little perishing strength that is in you.

Little enough, and perishing, often without reward, however well spent. Understand that Virtue does not consist in doing what will be presently paid, or even paid to all, to you, the virtuous person. It may so chance; or may not. It will be paid, some day; but the vital condition of it, as virtue, is that it shall be content in its own deed, and desirous rather that the pay of it, if any, should be for others; just as it is also the vital condition of vice to be content in its own deed, and desirous that the pay thereof, if any, should be to others.

You have probably heard of St. Louis before now:

and perhaps also that he built the Sainte Chapelle of
Paris, of which you may have seen that I wrote the
other day to the *Telegraph*, as being the most precious
piece of Gothic in Northern Europe ; but you are not
likely to have known that the spire of it was Tenterden
steeple over again, and the cause of fatal sands many,
quick, and slow, and above all, of the running of these in
the last hour-glass of France ; for that spire, and others
like it, subordinate, have acted ever since as lightning-
rods, in a reverse manner ; carrying, not the fire of heaven
innocently to earth, but electric fire of earth innocently
to heaven, leaving us all, down here, cold.   The best
virtue and heart-fire of France (not to say of England,
who building her towers for the most part with four
pinnacles instead of one, in a somewhat quadrumanous
type, finds them less apt as conductors), have spent
themselves for these past six centuries in running up
those steeples and off them, nobody knows where, leaving a " holy Republic " as residue at the bottom ; helpless, clay-cold, and croaking, a habitation of frogs, which
poor Garibaldi fights for, vainly raging against the ghost
of St. Louis.

It is of English ghosts, however, that I would fain
tell you somewhat to-day ; of them, and of the land
they haunt, and know still for theirs.   For hear this to
begin with :—

" While a map of France or Germany in the eleventh
century is useless for modern purposes, and looks like

the picture of another region, a map of England proper
in the reign of Victoria hardly differs at all from a map
of England proper in the reign of William " (the Con-
queror).   So says, very truly, Mr. Freeman in his *History
of the Conquest.*   Are there any of you who care for
this *old* England, of which the map has remained un-
changed for so long ?   I believe you would care more for
her, and less for yourselves, except as her faithful children,
if you knew a little more about her ; and especially more
of what she has been.   The difficulty, indeed, at any time,
is in finding out what she has been ; for that which people
usually call her history is not hers at all ; but that of her
Kings, or the tax-gatherers employed by them, which is
as if people were to call Mr. Gladstone's history, or
Mr. Lowe's, yours and mine.

But the history even of her Kings is worth reading.
You remember, I said, that sometimes in church it might
keep you awake to be told a little of it.   For a simple
instance, you have heard probably of Absalom's rebellion
against his father,-and of David's agony at his death, until
from very weariness you have ceased to feel the power of
the story.   You would not feel it less vividly if you knew
that a far more fearful sorrow, of the like kind, had
happened to one of your own Kings, perhaps the best
we have had, take him for all in all.   Not one only, but
three of his sons, rebelled against *him*, and were urged
into rebellion by their mother.   The Prince, who should
have been King after him, was pardoned, not once, but

many times—pardoned wholly, with rejoicing over him as over the dead alive, and set at his father's right hand in the kingdom ; but all in vain. Hard and treacherous to the heart's core, nothing wins him, nothing warns, nothing binds. He flies to France, and wars at last alike against father and brother, till, falling sick through mingled guilt, and shame, and rage, he repents idly as the fever-fire withers him. His father sends him the signet ring from his finger in token of one more forgiveness. The Prince lies down upon a heap of ashes with a halter round his neck, and so dies. When his father heard it he fainted away three times, and then broke out into bitterest crying and tears. This, you would have thought enough for the Third dark Fate to have appointed for a man's sorrows. It was little to that which was to come. His second son, who was now his Prince of England, conspired against him, and pursued his father from city to city, in Norman France. At last, even his youngest son, best beloved of all, abandoned him, and went over to his enemies.

This was enough. Between him and his children Heaven commanded its own peace. He sickened and died of grief on the oth of July, 1189.

The son who had killed him, " repented " now; but there could be no signet ring sent to him. Perhaps the dead do not forgive. Men say, as he stood by his father's corpse, that the blood burst from his nostrils. One child only had been faithful to him, but he was the son of a girl whom he had loved much, and as he should not ; his

Queen, therefore, being a much older person, and strict upon proprieties, poisoned her ; nevertheless poor Rosamond's son never failed him ; won a battle for him in England, which, in all human probability, saved his kingdom ; and was made a bishop, and turned out a bishop of the best.

· You know already a little about the Prince who stood unforgiven (as it seemed) by his father's body. He, also, had to forgive, in his time ; but only a stranger's arrow shot—not those reversed " arrows in the hand of the giant," by which his father died. Men called him " Lionheart," not untruly ; and the English as a people, have prided themselves somewhat ever since on having, every man of them, the heart of a lion ; without inquiring particularly either what sort of heart a lion has, or whether to have the heart of a lamb might not sometimes be more to the purpose. But it so happens that the name was very justly given to this prince ; and I want you to study his character somewhat, with me, because in all our history there is no truer representative of one great species of the British squire, under all the three significances of the name ; for this Richard of ours was beyond most of his fellows, a Rider and a Shieldbearer ; and beyond all men of his day, a Carver ; and in disposition and *un*reasonable exercise of intellectual power, typically a Squire altogether.

Note of him first, then, that he verily desired the good of his people (provided it could be contrived without any check of his own humour), and that he saw his way to it a great deal clearer than any of your squires do now. Here are some of his laws for you :—

" Having set forth the great inconveniences arising from the diversity of weights and measures in different parts of the kingdom, he, by a law, commanded all measures of corn, and other dry goods, as also of liquors, to be exactly the same in all his dominions ; and that the rim of each of these measures should be a circle of iron. By another law, he commanded all cloth to be woven two yards in breadth within the lists, and of equal goodness in all parts ; and that all cloth which did not answer this description should be seized and burnt. He enacted, further, that all the coin of the kingdom should be exactly of the same weight and fineness ;—that no Christian should take any interest for money lent ; and, to prevent the extortions of the Jews, he commanded that all compacts between Christians and Jews should be made in the presence of witnesses, and the conditions of them put in writing."   So, you see, in Cœur-de-Lion's day, it was not esteemed of absolute necessity to put agreements between *Christians* in writing !   Which if it were not now, you know we might save a great deal of money, and discharge some of our workmen round Temple Bar, as well as from Woolwich Dockyards.   Note also that bit about interest of money also for future reference.   In the next place observe that this King had great objection to thieves —at least to any person whom he clearly comprehended

to be a thief. He was the inventor of a mode of treat-
ment which I believe the Americans—among whom it
has not fallen altogether into disuse—do not gratefully
enough recognize as a Monarchical institution. By the
last of the laws for the government of his fleet in his
expedition to Palestine, it is decreed,—" That whosoever
is convicted of theft shall have his head shaved, melted
pitch poured upon it, and the feathers from a pillow
shaken over it, that he may be known ; and shall be
put on shore on the first land which the ship touches."
And not only so ; he even objected to any theft by
misrepresentation or deception,—for being evidently
particularly interested, like Mr. Mill, in that cloth manufacture, and having made the above law about the breadth
of the web, which has caused it to be spoken of ever
since as " Broad Cloth," and besides, for better preservation of its breadth, enacted that the Ell shall be of
the same length all over the kingdom, and that it shall
be made of iron—(so that Mr. Tennyson's provision for
National defences—that every shop-boy should strike
with his cheating yard-wand home, would be mended
much by the substitution of King Richard's *honest* ell-
wand, and for once with advisable encouragement to
the iron trade)—King Richard finally declares—" That
it shall be of the same goodness in the middle as at
the sides, and that no merchant in any part of the kingdom of England shall stretch before his shop or booth
a red or black cloth, or any other thing by which the

sight of buyers is frequently deceived in the choice of good cloth."

These being Richard's rough and unreasonable, chancing nevertheless, being wholly honest, to be wholly right, notions of business, the next point you are to note in him is his unreasonable good humour; an eminent character of English Squires; a very loveable one; and available to himself and others in many ways, but not altogether so exemplary as many think it. If you are unscrupulously resolved, whenever you can get your own way, to take it; if you are in a position of life wherein you can get a good deal of it, and if you have pugnacity enough to enjoy fighting with anybody who will not give it to you, there is little reason why you should ever be out of humour, unless indeed your way is a broad one, wherein you are like to be opposed in force. Richard's way was a very narrow one. To be first in battle, (generally obtaining that main piece of his will without question; once only worsted, by a French knight, and then not at all good-humouredly,) to be first in recognized command—therefore contending with his father, who was both in wisdom and acknowledged place superior; but scarcely contending at all with his brother John, who was as definitely and deeply beneath him; good-humoured unreasonably, while he was killing his father, the best of kings, and letting his brother rule unresisted, who was among the worst; and only proposing for his object in life to enjoy himself everywhere in a chivalrous, poetical, and pleasantly animal manner, as a strong man always may. What should he have been out of humour for? That he brightly and bravely lived through his captivity is much indeed to his honour ; but it was his point of honour to be bright and brave ; not at all to take care of his kingdom. A king who cared for that, would have got thinner and sadder in prison.

And it remains true of the English squire to this day, that, for the most part, he thinks that his kingdom is given him that he may be bright and brave ; and not at all that the sunshine or valour in him is meant to be of use to his kingdom.

But the next point you have to note in Richard is indeed a very noble quality, and true English ; he always does as much of his work as he can with his own hands. He was not in any wise a king who would sit by a windmill to watch his son and his men at work, though brave kings have done so. As much as might be, of whatever had to be done, he would stedfastly do from his own shoulder ; his main tool being an old Greek one, and the working God Vulcan's—the clearing axe. When that was no longer needful, and nothing would serve but spade and trowel, still the king was foremost ; and after the weary retreat to Ascalon, when he found the place " so completely ruined and deserted, that it afforded neither food, lodging, nor protection," nor any other sort of capital,—forthwith, 20th January, 1192—his army and he set to work to repair it ; a three months' business, of incessant toil, " from which the king himself was not exempted, but wrought with greater ardour than any common labourer."

The next point of his character is very English also, but less honourably so. I said but now that he had a great objection to anybody whom he clearly comprehended to be a thief. But he had great difficulty in reaching anything like an abstract definition of thieving, such as would include every method of it, and every culprit, which is an incapacity very common to many of us to this day. For instance, he carried off a great deal of treasure which belonged to his father, from Chinon (the royal treasury-town in France), and fortified his own castles in Poitou with it ; and when he wanted money to go crusading with, sold the royal castles, manors, woods, and forests, and even the superiority of the Crown of England over the kingdom of Scotland, which his father had wrought hard for, for about a hundred thousand pounds. Nay, the highest honours and most important offices become venal under him ; and from a Princess's dowry to a Saracen caravan, nothing comes much amiss ; not but that he gives generously also ; whole ships at a time when he is in the humour ; but his main practice is getting and spending, never saving ; which covetousness is at last the death of him. For hearing that a considerable treasure of ancient coins and medals has been found in the lands of Vidomar, Viscount of Limoges, King Richard sends forthwith to claim this waif for himself. The Viscount offers him part only,

presumably having an antiquarian turn of mind. Whereupon Richard loses his temper, and marches forthwith
with some Brabant men, mercenaries, to besiege the
Viscount in his castle of Chalus ; proposing, first, to
possess himself of the antique and otherwise interesting
coin in the castle, and then, on his general principle of
objection to thieves, to hang the garrison. The garrison,
on this, offer to give up the antiquities if they may march
off themselves ; but Richard declares that nothing will
serve but they must all be hanged. Whereon the siege
proceeding by rule, and Richard looking, as usual, into
matters with his own eyes, and going too near the walls,
an arrow well meant, though half spent, pierces the strong
white shoulder ; the shield-bearing one, carelessly forward
above instead of under shield ; or perhaps, rather, when he
was afoot, shieldless, engineering. He finishes his work,
however, though the scratch teases him ; plans his assault,
carries his castle, and duly hangs his garrison, all but the
archer, whom in his royal, unreasoning way he thinks
better of, for the well-spent arrow. But he pulls it out
impatiently, and the head of it stays in the fair flesh ; a
little surgery follows ; not so skilful as the archery of
those days, and the lion heart is appeased—

Sixth April, 1199.

We will pursue our historical studies, if you please, in
that month of the present year. But I wish, in the meantime, you would observe, and meditate on, the quite
Anglican character of Richard, to his death.

It might have been remarked to him, on his projecting the expedition to Chalus, that there were not a few Roman coins, and other antiquities, to be found in his own kingdom of England, without fighting for them, but by mere spade labour and other innocuous means ; —that even the brightest new money was obtainable from his loyal people in almost any quantity for civil asking ; and that the same loyal people, encouraged and protected, and above all, kept clean-handed, in the arts, by their king, might produce treasures more covetable than any antiquities.

"No ;" Richard would have answered,—"that is all hypothetical and visionary ; here is a pot of coin presently to be had—no doubt about it—inside the walls here :—let me once get hold of that, and then,"—

  *   *   *   *   *

That is what we English call being " Practical."

Believe me,

Faithfully yours,

JOHN RUSKIN.

FORS CLAVIGERA.

LETTER THE 4th.

SWITCHES OF BROOM.

DENMARK HILL,
1st April, 1871.

MY FRIENDS,

It cannot but be pleasing to us to reflect, this day, that if we are often foolish enough to talk English without understanding it, we are often wise enough to talk Latin without knowing it. For this month retains its pretty Roman name, and means the month of Opening; of the light in the days, and the life in the leaves, and of the voices of birds, and of the hearts of men.

And being the month of Manifestation, it is preeminently the month of Fools;—for under the beatific influences of moral sunshine, or Education, the Fools always come out first.

But what is less pleasing to reflect upon, this spring morning, is, that there are some kinds of education which may be described, not as moral sunshine, but as moral moonshine; and that, under these, Fools come out both First—and Last.

IV.

We have, it seems, now set our opening hearts much on this one point, that we will have education for all men and women now, and for all boys and girls that are to be. Nothing, indeed, can be more desirable, if only we determine also what kind of education we are to have. It is taken for granted that any education must be good ;—that the more of it we get, the better ; that bad education only means little education ; and that the worst thing we have to fear is getting none. Alas, that is not at all so. Getting no education is by no means the worst thing that can happen to us. One of the pleasantest friends I ever had in my life was a Savoyard guide, who could only read with difficulty, and write scarcely intelligibly, and by great effort. He knew no language but his own—no science, except as much practical agriculture as served him to till his fields. But he was, without exception, one of the happiest persons, and, on the whole, one of the best, I have ever known : and after lunch, when he had had his half bottle of Savoy wine, he would generally, as we walked up some quiet valley in the afternoon light, give me a little lecture on philosophy ; and after I had fatigued and provoked him with less cheerful views of the world than his own, he would fall back to my servant behind me, and console himself with a shrug of the shoulders, and a whispered " Le paúvre enfant, il ne sait pas vivre ! "—(" The poor child, he doesn't know how to live.")

No, my friends, believe me, it is not the going without education at all that we have most to dread. The real thing to be feared is getting a bad one. There are all sorts—good, and very good ; bad, and very bad. The children of rich people often get the worst education that is to be had for money ; the children of the poor often get the best for nothing. And you have really these two things now to decide for yourselves in England before you can take one quite safe practical step in the matter, namely, first, what a good education is ; and, secondly, who is likely to give it you.

What it is ? " Everybody knows that," I suppose you would most of you answer. " Of course—to be taught to read, and write, and cast accounts ; and to learn geography, and geology, and astronomy, and chemistry, and German, and French, and Italian, and Latin, and Greek and the aboriginal Aryan language."

Well, when you had learned all that, what would you do next ? " Next ? Why then we should be perfectly happy, and make as much money as ever we liked, and we would turn out our toes before any company." I am not sure myself, and I don't think you can be, of any one of these three things. At least, as to making you very happy, I know something, myself, of nearly all these matters—not much, but still quite as much as most men, under the ordinary chances of life, with a fair education, are likely to get together—and I assure you the knowledge does not make me happy at all. When I was a boy I used to like seeing the sun rise. I didn't know, then, there were any spots on the sun ; now I do, and am always frightened lest any more should come.

When I was a boy, I used to care about pretty stones. I got some Bristol diamonds at Bristol, and some dog-tooth spar in Derbyshire ; my whole collection had cost, perhaps, three half-crowns, and was worth considerably less ; and I knew nothing whatever, rightly, about any single stone in it ;—could not even spell their names : but words cannot tell the joy they used to give me. Now, I have a collection of minerals worth perhaps from two to three thousand pounds ; and I know more about some of them than most other people. But I am not a whit happier, either for my knowledge, or possessions, for other geologists dispute my theories, to my grievous indignation and discontentment ; and I am miserable about all my best specimens, because there are better in the British Museum.

No, I assure you, knowledge by itself will not make you happy ; still less will it make you rich. Perhaps you thought I was writing carelessly when I told you, last month, " science did not pay." But you don't know what science is. You fancy it means mechanical art ; and so you have put a statue of Science on the Holborn Viaduct, with a steam-engine regulator in its hands. My ingenious friends, science has no more to do with making steam-engines than with making breeches; though she condescends to help you a little in such necessary (or it may be, con-ceivably, in both cases, sometimes unnecessary) businesses. Science lives only in quiet places, and with odd people, mostly poor. Mr. John Kepler, for instance, who is found by Sir Henry Wotton " in the picturesque green country

by the shores of the Donau, in a little black tent in a
field, convertible, like a windmill, to all quarters, a
camera-obscura, in fact. Mr. John invents rude toys,
writes almanacks, practises medicine, for good reasons,
his encouragement from the Holy Roman Empire and
mankind being a pension of 18*l.* a year and that hardly
ever paid."* This is what one gets by star-gazing, my
friends. And you cannot be simple enough, even in
April, to think I got my three thousand pounds'-worth
of minerals by studying mineralogy? Not so; they were
earned for me by hard labour; my father's in England,
and many a sun-burnt vineyard-dresser's in Spain.

"What business had you, in your idleness, with their
earnings then?" you will perhaps ask. None, it may be;
I will tell you in a little while how you may find that out;
it is not to the point now. But it is to the point that
you should observe I have not kept their earnings, the
portion of them, at least, with which I bought minerals.
That part of their earnings is all gone to feed the miners
in Cornwall, or on the Hartz mountains, and I have only
got for myself a few pieces of glittering (not always that,
but often unseemly) stone, which neither vine-dressers nor
miners cared for; which you yourselves would have to learn
many hard words, much cramp mathematics, and useless
chemistry, in order to care for; which, if ever you did
care for, as I do, would most likely only make you envious
of the British Museum, and occasionally uncomfortable
if any harm happened to your dear stones. I have a

* Carlyle, *Frederick*, vol. i. p. 321 (first edition).

piece of red oxide of copper, for instance, which grieves me poignantly by losing its colour; and a crystal of sulphide of lead, with a chip in it, which causes me a great deal of concern—in April; because I see it then by the fresh sunshine.

My oxide of copper and sulphide of lead you will not then wisely envy me. Neither, probably, would you covet a handful of hard brown gravel, with a rough pebble in it, whitish, and about the size of a pea; nor a few grains of apparently brass filings, with which the gravel is mixed. I was but a fool to give good money for such things, you think? It may well be. I gave thirty pounds for that handful of gravel, and the miners who found it were ill-paid then; and it is not clear to me that this produce of their labour was the best possible. Shall we consider of it, with the help of the Cambridge Catechism? at the tenth page of which you will find that Mr. Mill's definition of productive labour is—" That which produces utilities fixed and embodied in material objects."

This is very fine—indeed, superfine—English; but I can, perhaps, make the meaning of the Greatest Thinker in England a little more lucid for you by vulgarizing his terms.

" Object,' 'you must always remember, is fine English for " Thing." It is a semi-Latin word, and properly means a thing " thrown in your way;" so that if you put " ion " to the end of it, it becomes Objection. We will rather say " Thing," if you have no objection—you and I. A " Material " thing, then, of course, signifies something solid and tangible. It is very necessary for Political Economists always to insert this word "material," lest people should suppose that there was any use or value in Thought or Knowledge, and other such immaterial objects.

"Embodied" is a particularly elegant word ; but superfluous, because you know it would not be possible that a Utility should be disembodied, as long as it was in a material object. But when you wish to express yourself as thinking in a great manner, you may say— as, for instance, when you are supping vegetable soup— that your power of doing so conveniently and gracefully is "Embodied" in a spoon.

"Fixed" is, I am afraid, rashly, as well as super-fluously, introduced into his definition by Mr. Mill. It is conceivable that some Utilities may be also volatile, or planetary, even when embodied. But at last we come to the great word in the great definition—"Utility."

And this word, I am sorry to say, puzzles me most of all ; for I never myself saw a Utility, either out of the body, or in it, and should be much embarrassed if ordered to produce one in either state.

But it is fortunate for us that all this seraphic lan-guage, reduced to the vulgar tongue, will become, though fallen in dignity and reduced in dimension, perfectly intelligible. The Greatest Thinker in England means by these beautiful words to tell you that Productive labour is labour that produces a Useful Thing. Which, indeed, perhaps, you knew—or, without the assistance of great

thinkers, might have known, before now. But if Mr. Mill
had said so much, simply, you might have been tempted
to ask farther—"What things are useful, and what are
not?" And as Mr. Mill does not know, nor any other
Political Economist going,—and as they therefore particularly wish nobody to ask them,—it is convenient to
say instead of "useful things," "utilities fixed and embodied in material objects," because that sounds so very
like complete and satisfactory information, that one is
ashamed, after getting it, to ask for any more.

But it is not, therefore, less discouraging that for the
present I have got no help towards discovering whether
my handful of gravel with the white pebble in it was
worth my thirty pounds or not. I am afraid it is not
a useful thing to *me*. It lies at the back of a drawer,
locked up all the year round. I never look at it now,
for I know all about it : the only satisfaction I have for
my money is knowing that nobody else can look at it ;
and if nobody else wanted to, I shouldn't even have that.

"What did you buy it for, then?" you will ask. Well,
if you must have the truth, because I was a Fool, and
wanted it. Other people have bought such things before
me. The white stone is a diamond, and the apparent
brass filings are gold dust ; but, I admit, nobody ever yet
wanted such things who was in his right senses. Only
now, as I have candidly answered all your questions, will
you answer one of mine? If I hadn't bought it, what
would you have had me do with my money? Keep *that*
in the drawer instead?—or at my banker's, till it grew out

of thirty pounds into sixty and a hundred, in fulfilment
of the law respecting seed sown in good ground ?

Doubtless, that would have been more meritorious for
the time. But when I had got the sixty or the hundred
pounds—what should I have done with *them ?* The
question only becomes doubly and trebly serious; and all
the more, to me, because when I told you last January
that I had bought a picture for a thousand pounds,
permitting myself in that folly for your advantage, as I
thought, hearing that many of you wanted art Patronage,
and wished to live by painting,—one of your own popular
organs, the *Liverpool Daily Courier*, of February 9th, said,
" it showed want of taste,—of tact," and was " something
like a mockery," to tell you so ! I am not to buy pictures,
therefore, it seems ;—you like to be kept in mines and
tunnels, and occasionally blown hither and thither, or
crushed flat, rather than live by painting, in good light,
and with the chance of remaining all day in a whole
and unextended skin ? But what *shall* I buy, then, with
the next thirty pieces of gold I can scrape together ?
Precious things have been bought, indeed, and sold,
before now for thirty pieces, even of silver, but with
doubtful issue. The over-charitable person who was
bought to be killed at that price, indeed, advised the
giving of alms ; but you won't have alms, I suppose, you
are so independent, nor go into almshouses—(and, truly,
I did not much wonder, as I walked by the old church
of Abingdon, a Sunday or two since, where the almshouses are set round the churchyard, and under the level

of it, and with a cheerful view of it, except that the
tombstones slightly block the light of the lattice-windows;
with beautiful texts from Scripture over the doors, to
remind the paupers still more emphatically that, highly
blessed as they were, they were yet mortal)—you won't
go into almshouses; and all the clergy in London have
been shrieking against almsgiving to the lower poor this
whole winter long, till I am obliged, whenever I want to
give anybody a penny, to look up and down the street
first, to see if a clergyman's coming. Of course, I know
I might buy as many iron railings as I please, and be
praised; but I've no room for them. I can't well burn
more coals than I do, because of the blacks, which spoil
my books; and the Americans won't let me buy any
blacks alive, or else I would have some black dwarfs with
parrots, such as one sees in the pictures of Paul Veronese.
I should, of course, like myself, above all things, to buy
a pretty white girl, with a title—and I could get great
praise for doing that—only I haven't money enough.
White girls come dear, even when one buys them only
like coals, for fuel. The Duke of Bedford, indeed, bought
Joan of Arc from the French, to burn, for only ten
thousand pounds, and a pension of three hundred a year
to the Bastard of Vendome—and I could and would
have given that for her, and not burnt her; but one hasn't
such a chance every day. *Will* you, any of you, have
the goodness—beggars, clergymen, workmen, seraphic
doctors, Mr. Mill, Mr. Fawcett, or the Politico-Economic
Professor of my own University—I challenge you, I

beseech you, all and singly, to tell me what I am to do with my money.

I mean, indeed, to give you my own poor opinion on the subject in May ; though I feel the more embarrassed in the thought of doing so, because, in this present April, I am so much a fool as not even to know clearly whether I have got any money or not. I know, indeed, that things go on at present as if I had ; but it seems to me that there must be a mistake somewhere, and that some day it will be found out. For instance, I have seven thousand pounds in what we call the Funds or Founded things ; but I am not comfortable about the Founding of them. All that I can see of them is a square bit of paper, with some ugly printing on it, and all that I know of them is that this bit of paper gives me a right to tax you every year, and make you pay me two hundred pounds out of your wages ; which is very pleasant for me : but how long will you be pleased to do so ? Suppose it should occur to you, any summer's day, that you had better not ? Where would my seven thousand pounds be ? In fact, where are they now ? We call ourselves a rich people ; but you see this seven thousand pounds of mine has no real existence ; —it only means that you, the workers, are poorer by two hundred pounds a year than you would be if I hadn't got it. And this is surely a very odd kind of money for a country to boast of. Well, then, besides this, I have a bit of low land at Greenwich, which, as far as I see anything of it, is not money at all, but only mud ; and would be of as little use to me as my handful of gravel in the drawer, if it were not that an ingenious person has found out that he can make chimney-pots of it ; and, every quarter, he brings me fifteen pounds off the price of his chimney-pots, so that I am always sympathetically glad when there's a high wind, because then I know my ingenious friend's business is thriving. But suppose it should come into his head, in any less windy month than this April, that he had better bring me none of the price of his chimneys ? And even though he should go on, as I hope he will, patiently,—(and I always give him a glass of wine when he brings me the fifteen pounds),—is this really to be called money of mine ? And is the country any richer because, when anybody's chimney-pot is blown down in Greenwich, he must pay something extra, to me, before he can put it on again ?

Then, also, I have some houses in Marylebone, which though indeed very ugly and miserable, yet, so far as they are actual beams and brick-bats put into shape, I might have imagined to be real property ; only, you know, Mr. Mill says that people who build houses don't produce a commodity, but only do us a service. So I suppose my houses are not " utilities embodied in material objects" (and indeed they don't look much like it) ; but I know I have the right to keep anybody from living in them unless they pay me ; only suppose some day the Irish faith, that people ought to be lodged for nothing, should become an English one also—where would my money be ? Where is it now, except as a chronic abstraction from other people's earnings ?

So again, I have some land in Yorkshire—some Bank
" Stock " (I don't in the least know what *that* is)—and
the like ; but whenever I examine into these possessions,
I find they melt into one or another form of future taxation, and that I am always sitting (if I were working I
shouldn't mind, but I am only sitting) at the receipt of
Custom, and a Publican as well as a sinner.   And then
to embarrass the business further yet, I am quite at
variance with other people about the place where this
money, whatever it is, comes from.   The *Spectator*, for
instance, in its article of 25th June of last year, on Mr.
Goschen's " lucid and forcible speech of Friday-week,"
says that " the country is once more getting rich, and the
money is filtering downwards to the actual workers."   But
whence, then, did it filter down to us, the actual idlers ?
This is really a question very appropriate for April.   For
such golden rain raineth *not* every day, but in a showery
and capricious manner, out of heaven, upon us ; mostly,
as far as I can judge, rather pouring down than filtering
upon idle persons, and running in thinner driblets, but I
hope purer for the filtering process, to the "actual workers."
But where *does* it come from ? and in the times of drought
between the showers, where does it go to ?   " The country
is getting rich again," says the *Spectator;* but then, if the
April clouds fail, may it get poor again ?   And when it
again becomes poor,—when, last 25th of June, it *was*
poor,—what becomes, or had become, of the money ?
Was it verily lost, or only torpid in the winter of our
discontent ? or was it sown and buried in corruption, to

be raised in a multifold power ?   When we are in a panic
about our money, what do we think is going to happen
to it ?   Can no economist teach us to keep it safe after we
have once got it ? nor any " beloved physician "—as I read
the late Sir James Simpson is called in Edinburgh—guard
even our solid gold against death, or at least, fits of an
apoplectic character, alarming to the family ?

All these questions trouble me greatly ; but still to me
the strangest point in the whole matter is, that though
we idlers always speak as if we were enriched by Heaven,
and became ministers of its bounty to *you ;* if ever you
think the ministry slack, and take to definite pillage of
us, no good ever comes of it to you ; but the sources
of wealth seem to be stopped instantly, and you are
reduced to the small gain of making gloves of our skins ;
while, on the contrary, as long as we continue pillaging
you, there seems no end to the profitableness of the
business ; but always, however bare we strip you, presently, more, to be had.   For instance—just read this
little bit out of Froissart—about the English army in
France before the battle of Crecy :—

" We will now return to the expedition of the King of England.
Sir Godfrey de Harcourt, as marshal, advanced before the King,
with the vanguard of five hundred armed men and two thousand
archers, and rode on for six or seven leagues' distance from the
main army, burning and destroying the country.   They found it
rich and plentiful, abounding in all things ; the barns full of
every sort of corn, and the houses with riches : the inhabitants
at their ease, having cars, carts, horses, swine, sheep, and everything in abundance which the country afforded.   They seized
whatever they chose of all these good things, and brought them

to the King's army; but the soldiers did not give any account
to their officers, or to those appointed by the King, of the gold
and silver they took, which they kept to themselves. When they
were come back, with all their booty safely packed in waggons,
the Earl of Warwick, the Earl of Suffolk, the Lord Thomas
Holland, and the Lord Reginald Cobham, took their march,
with their battalion on the right, burning and destroying the
country in the same way that Sir Godfrey de Harcourt was
doing. The King marched, with the main body, between these
two battalions; and every night they all encamped together.
The King of England and Prince of Wales had, in their battalion,
about three thousand men-at-arms, six thousand archers, ten
thousand infantry, without counting those that were under the
marshals; and they marched on in the manner I have before
mentioned, burning and destroying the country, but without
breaking their line of battle. They did not turn towards
Coutances, but advanced to St. Lo, in Coutantin, which in
those days was a very rich and commercial town, and worth
three such towns as Coutances. In the town of St. Lo was
much drapery, and many wealthy inhabitants; among them you
might count eight or nine score that were engaged in commerce.
When the King of England was come near to the town, he
encamped; he would not lodge in it for fear of fire. He sent,
therefore, his advanced guard forward, who soon conquered it,
at a trifling loss, and completely plundered it. No one can
imagine the quantity of riches they found in it, nor the number
of bales of cloth. If there had been any purchasers, they might
have bought enough at a very cheap rate.

"The English then advanced towards Caen, which is a much
larger town, stronger, and fuller of draperies and all other sorts
of merchandize, rich citizens, noble dames and damsels, and fine
churches.

"On this day (Froissart does not say what day) the English
rose very early, and made themselves ready to march to Caen :
the King heard mass before sunrise, and afterwards mounting
his horse, with the Prince of Wales, and Sir Godfrey de Harcourt

(who was marshal and director of the army), marched forward in order of battle. The battalion of the marshals led the van, and came near to the handsome town of Caen.

"When the townsmen, who had taken the field, perceived the English advancing, with banners and pennons flying in abundance, and saw those archers whom they had not been accustomed to, they were so frightened that they betook themselves to flight, and ran for the town in great disorder.

"The English, who were after the runaways, made great havoc; for they spared none.

"Those inhabitants who had taken refuge in the garrets, flung down from them, in these narrow streets, stones, benches, and whatever they could lay hands on; so that they killed and wounded upwards of five hundred of the English, which so enraged the King of England, when he received the reports in the evening, that he ordered the remainder of the inhabitants to be put to the sword, and the town burnt. But Sir Godfrey de Harcourt said to him : 'Dear sir, assuage somewhat of your anger, and be satisfied with what has already been done. You have a long journey yet to make before you arrive at Calais, whither it is your intention to go : and there are in this town a great number of inhabitants, who will defend themselves obstinately in their houses, if you force them to it : besides, it will cost you many lives before the town can be destroyed, which may put a stop to your expedition to Calais, and it will not redound to your honour : therefore be sparing of your men, for in a month's time you will have call for them.' The King replied : 'Sir Godfrey, you are our marshal; therefore order as you please; for this time we wish not to interfere.'

"Sir Godfrey then rode through the streets, his banner displayed before him, and ordered, in the King's name, that no one should dare, under pain of immediate death, to insult or hurt man or woman of the town, or attempt to set fire to any part of it. Several of the inhabitants, on hearing this proclamation, received the English into their houses; and others opened their coffers to them, giving up their all, since they were assured of their lives. However, there were, in spite of these orders, many atrocious thefts and murders committed. The English continued masters of the town for three days; in this time, they amassed great wealth, which they sent in barges down the river of Estreham, to St. Sauveur, two leagues off, where their fleet was. The Earl of Huntingdon made preparations therefore, with the two hundred men-at-arms and his four hundred archers, to carry over to England their riches and prisoners. The King purchased, from Sir Thomas Holland and his companions, the constable of France and the Earl of Tancarville, and paid down twenty thousand nobles for them.

" When the King had finished his business in Caen, and sent his fleet to England, loaded with cloths, jewels, gold and silver plate, and a quantity of other riches, and upwards of sixty knights, with three hundred able citizens, prisoners; he then left his quarters and continued his march as before, his two marshals on his right and left, burning and destroying all the flat country. He took the road to Evreux, but found he could not gain anything there, as it was well fortified. He went on towards another town called Louviers, which was in Normandy, and where there were many manufactories of cloth : it was rich and commercial. The English won it easily, as it was not inclosed ; and having entered the town, it was plundered without opposition. They collected much wealth there; and, after they had done what they pleased, they marched on into the county of Evreux, where they burnt everything except the fortified towns and castles, which the King left unattacked, as he was desirous of sparing his men and artillery. He therefore made for the banks of the Seine, in his approach to Rouen, where there were plenty of men-at-arms from Normandy, under the command of the Earl of Harcourt, brother to Sir Godfrey, and the Earl of Dreux.

" The English did not march direct towards Rouen, but went to Gisors, which has a strong castle, and burnt the town. After this, they destroyed Vernon, and all the country between Rouen and Pont-de-l'Arche : they then came to Mantes and Meulan, which they treated in the same manner, and ravaged all the country round about.

" They passed by the strong castle of Roulleboise, and everywhere found the bridges on the Seine broken down. They pushed forward until they came to Poissy, where the bridge was also destroyed; but the beams and other parts of it were lying in the river.

"The King of England remained at the nunnery of Poissy to the middle of August, and celebrated there the feast of the Virgin Mary."

It all reads at first, you see, just like a piece out of the newspapers of last month; but there are material differences, notwithstanding. We fight inelegantly as well as expensively, with machines instead of bow and spear; we kill about a thousand now to the score then, in settling any quarrel—(Agincourt was won with the loss of less than a hundred men; only 25,000 English altogether were engaged at Crecy; and 12,000, some say only 8,000, at Poictiers); we kill with far ghastlier wounds, crashing bones and flesh together; we leave our wounded necessarily for days and nights in heaps on the fields of battle; we pillage districts twenty times as large, and with completer destruction of more valuable property; and with a destruction as irreparable as it is complete; for if the French or English burnt a church one day, they could build a prettier one the next; but the modern Prussians couldn't even build so much as an imitation of one; we rob on credit, by requisition, with ingenious mercantile prolongations of claim; and we improve contention of arms with contention of tongues, and are able to multiply the rancour of cowardice, and mischief of lying, in universal and permanent print; and so we lose our tempers as well as our money, and become

indecent in behaviour as in raggedness ; for, whereas, in
old times, two nations separated by a little pebbly stream
like the Tweed, or even the two halves of one nation,
separated by thirty fathoms' depth of salt water (for
most of the English knights and all the English kings
were French by race, and the best of them by birth
also)—would go on pillaging and killing each other
century after century, without the slightest ill-feeling
towards, or disrespect for, one another,—we can neither
give anybody a beating courteously, nor take one in
good part, or without screaming and lying about it : and
finally, we add to these perfected Follies of Action more
finely perfected Follies of Inaction ; and contrive hitherto
unheard-of ways of being wretched through the very
abundance of peace ; our workmen, here, vowing themselves to idleness, lest they should lower Wages, and
there, being condemned by their parishes to idleness lest
they should lower Prices ; while outside the workhouse
all the parishioners are buying anything nasty, so that
it be cheap ; and, in a word, under the seraphic teaching
of Mr. Mill, we have determined at last that it is not
Destruction, but Production, that is the cause of human
distress ; and the "Mutual and Co-operative Colonization
Company" declares, ungrammatically, but distinctly, in its
circular sent to me on the 13th of last month, as a matter
universally admitted, even among Cabinet Ministers—
"that it is in the greater increasing power of production
and distribution as compared with demand, enabling the
few to do the work of many, that the active cause of the

wide-spread poverty among the producing and lower-middle classes lay, which entails such enormous burdens on the Nation, and exhibits our boasted progress in the light of a monstrous Sham."

Nevertheless, however much we have magnified and multiplied the follies of the past, the primal and essential principles of pillage have always been accepted; and from the days when England lay so waste under that worthy and economical King who " called his tailor lown," that " whole families, after sustaining life as long as they could by eating roots, and the flesh of dogs and horses, at last died of hunger, and you might see many pleasant villages without a single inhabitant of either sex," while little Harry Switch-of-Broom sate learning to spell in Bristol Castle, (taught, I think, properly by his good uncle the preceptorial use of his name-plant, though they say the first Harry was the finer clerk,) and his mother, dressed all in white, escaped from Oxford over the snow in the moonlight, through Bagley Wood here to Abingdon ; and under the snows, by Woodstock, the buds were growing for the bower of his Rose,—from that day to this, when the villages round Paris, and food-supply, are, by the blessing of God, as they then were round London—Kings have for the most part desired to win that pretty name of " Switch-of-Broom " rather by habit of growing in waste places; or even emulating the Vision of Dion in " sweeping—diligently sweeping," than by attaining the other virtue of the Planta Genista, set forth by Virgil and Pliny, that it is pliant, and

rich in honey ; the Lion-hearts of them seldom proving
profitable to you, even so much as the stomach of
Samson's Lion, or rendering it a soluble enigma in our
Israel, that "out of the eater came forth meat ;" nor
has it been only your Kings who have thus made you
pay for their guidance through the world, but your eccle-
siastics have also made you pay for guidance out of it—
particularly when it grew dark, and the signpost was
illegible where the upper and lower roads divided ;—so
that as far as I can read or calculate, dying has been
even more expensive to you than living ; and then, to
finish the business, as your virtues have been made costly
to you by the clergyman, so your vices have been made
costly to you by the lawyers ; and you have one entire
learned profession living on your sins, and the other on
your repentance. So that it is no wonder that, things
having gone on thus for a long time, you begin to think
that you would rather live as sheep without any shepherd,
and that having paid so dearly for your instruction in
religion and law, you should now set your hope on a
state of instruction in Irreligion and Liberty, which is,
indeed, a form of education to be had for nothing, alike
by the children of the Rich and Poor ; the saplings of
the tree that was to be desired to make us wise, growing
now in copsewood on the hills, or even by the roadsides,
in a Republican-Plantagenet manner, blossoming into
cheapest gold, either for coins, which of course you
Republicans will call, not Nobles, but Ignobles ; or crowns,
second and third hand—(head, I should say)—supplied

punctually on demand, with liberal reduction on quantity ;
the roads themselves beautifully public—tramwayed, perhaps—and with gates set open enough for all **men** to the
free, outer, better world, your chosen guide preceding you
merrily, thus—

with music and dancing.

You have always danced too willingly, poor friends, to
that player on the viol. We will try to hear, far away,
a faint note or two from a more chief musician on stringed
instruments, in May, when the time of the Singing of Birds
is come.

Faithfully yours,

JOHN RUSKIN.

FORS CLAVIGERA.

LETTER THE 5th.

WHITETHORN BLOSSOM.

" For lo, the winter is past,
The rain is over and gone,
The flowers appear on the earth,
The time of the singing of birds is come,
Arise, O my fair one, my dove,
And come."

DENMARK HILL,
1st *May*, 1871.

MY FRIENDS,

It has been asked of me, very justly, why I have hitherto written to you of things you were little likely to care for, in words which it was difficult for you to understand.

I have no fear but that you will one day understand all my poor words,—the saddest of them perhaps too well. But I have great fear that you may never come to understand these written above, which are part of a king's love-song, in one sweet May, of many long since gone.

I fear that for you the wild winter's rain may never

pass,—the flowers never appear on the earth ;—that for you no bird may ever sing ;—for you no perfect Love arise, and fulfil your life in peace.

" And why not for us, as for others ? " will you answer me so, and take my fear for you as an insult ?

Nay, it is no insult ;—nor am I happier than you.   For me, the birds do not sing, nor ever will.   But they would, for you, if you cared to have it so.   When I told you that you would never understand that love-song, I meant only that you would not desire to understand it.

Are you again indignant with me ?   Do you think, though you should labour, and grieve, and be trodden down in dishonour all your days, at least you can keep that one joy of Love, and that one honour of Home ? Had you, indeed, kept that, you had kept all.   But no men yet, in the history of the race, have lost it so piteously.   In many a country, and many an age, women have been compelled to labour for their husbands' wealth, or bread ; but never until now were they so homeless as to say, like the poor Samaritan, " I have no husband." Women of every country and people have sustained without complaint the labour of fellowship : for the women of the latter days in England it has been reserved to claim the privilege of isolation.

This, then, is the end of your universal education and civilization, and contempt of the ignorance of the Middle Ages, and of their chivalry.   Not only do you declare yourselves too indolent to labour for daughters and wives, and too poor to support them ; but you have made the neglected and distracted creatures hold it for an honour to be independent of you, and shriek for some hold of the mattock for themselves. Believe it or not, as you may, there has not been so low a level of thought reached by any race, since they grew to be male and female out of star-fish, or chickweed, or whatever else they have been made from, by natural selection,—according to modern science.

That modern science also, Economic and of other kinds, has reached its climax at last. For it seems to be the appointed function of the nineteenth century to exhibit in all things the elect pattern of perfect Folly, for a warning to the farthest future. Thus the statement of principle which I quoted to you in my last letter, from the circular of the Emigration Society, that it is over-production which is the cause of distress, is accurately the most foolish thing, not only hitherto ever said by men, but which it is possible for men ever to say, respecting their own business. It is a kind of opposite pole (or negative acme of mortal stupidity) to Newton's discovery of gravitation as an acme of mortal wisdom : —as no wise being on earth will ever be able to make such another wise discovery, so no foolish being on earth will ever be capable of saying such another foolish thing, through all the ages.

And the same crisis has been exactly reached by our natural science and by our art. It has several times

chanced to me, since I began these papers, to have the
exact thing shown or brought to me that I wanted for
illustration, just in time*—and it happened that on the
very day on which I published my last letter, I had to
go to the Kensington Museum ; and there I saw the most
perfectly and roundly ill-done thing which, as yet, in my
whole life I ever saw produced by art. It had a tablet
in front of it, bearing this inscription,—

"Statue in black and white marble, a Newfoundland Dog standing on
a Serpent, which rests on a marble cushion, the pedestal ornamented with
pietra dura fruits in relief.—*English. Present Century.* No. I."

It was so very right for me, the Kensington people
having been good enough to number it " I.," the thing
itself being almost incredible in its one-ness ; and, indeed,
such a punctual accent over the iota of Miscreation,—so
absolutely and exquisitely miscreant, that I am not myself
capable of conceiving a Number two, or three, or any
rivalship or association with it whatsoever. The extremity
of its unvirtue consisted, observe, mainly in the quantity
of instruction which was abused in it. It showed that the
persons who produced it had seen everything, and prae-
tised everything ; and misunderstood everything they saw,
and misapplied everything they did. They had seen

---

* Here is another curious instance : I have but a minute ago finished
correcting these sheets, and take up the *Times* of this morning, April 21st,
and find in it the suggestion by the Chancellor of the Exchequer for the
removal of exemption from taxation, of Agricultural horses and carts, in the
very nick of time to connect it, as a proposal for economic practice, with the
statement of economic principle respecting Production, quoted on last page.

Roman work, and Florentine work, and Byzantine work, and Gothic work ; and misunderstanding of everything had passed through them as the mud does through earthworms, and here at last was their worm-cast of a Production.

But the second chance that came to me that day, was more significant still. From the Kensington Museum I went to an afternoon tea, at a house where I was sure to meet some nice people. And among the first I met was an old friend who had been hearing some lectures on botany at the Kensington Museum, and been delighted by them. She is the kind of person who gets good out of everything, and she was quite right in being delighted ; besides that, as I found by her account of them, the lectures were really interesting, and pleasantly given. She had expected botany to be dull, and had not found it so, and " had learned so much." On hearing this, I proceeded naturally to inquire what ; for my idea of her was that before she went to the lectures at all, she had known more botany than she was likely to learn by them. So she told me that she had learned first of all that " there were seven sorts of leaves." Now I have always a great suspicion of the number Seven ; because when I wrote the Seven Lamps of Architecture, it required all the ingenuity I was master of to prevent them from becoming Eight, or even Nine, on my hands. So I thought to myself that it would be very charming if there were only seven sorts of leaves ; but that, perhaps, if one

looked the woods and forests of the world carefully
through, it was just possible that one might discover as
many as eight sorts ; and then where would my friend's
new knowledge of Botany be ? So I said, " That was
very pretty ; but what more ? " Then my friend told me
that she had no idea, before, that petals were leaves.
On which, I thought to myself that it would not have
been any great harm to her if she had remained under
her old impression that petals were petals. But I said,
" That was very pretty, too ; and what more ? " So
then my friend told me that the lecturer said, " the
object of his lectures would be entirely accomplished
if he could convince his hearers that there was no such
thing as a flower." Now, in that sentence you have
the most perfect and admirable summary given you of
the general temper and purposes of modern science.
It gives lectures on Botany, of which the object is to
show that there is no such thing as a flower ; on
Humanity, to show that there is no such thing as a
Man ; and on Theology, to show there is no such thing
as a God. No such thing as a Man, but only a
Mechanism ; no such thing as a God, but only a series
of forces. The two faiths are essentially one : if you
feel yourself to be only a machine, constructed to be a
Regulator of minor machinery, you will put your statue
of such science on your Holborn Viaduct, and necessarily
recognize only major machinery as regulating *you*.

I must explain the real meaning to you, however,

of that saying of the Botanical lecturer, for it has a wide bearing. Some fifty years ago the poet Goethe discovered that all the parts of plants had a kind of common nature, and would change into each other. Now this was a true discovery, and a notable one ; and you will find that, in fact, all plants are composed of essentially two parts—the leaf and root—one loving the light, the other darkness ; one liking to be clean, the other to be dirty ; one liking to grow for the most part up, the other for the most part down ; and each having faculties and purposes of its own. But the pure one which loves the light has, above all things, the purpose of being married to another leaf, and having child-leaves, and children's children of leaves, to make the earth fair for ever. And when the leaves marry, they put on wedding-robes, and are more glorious than Solomon in all his glory, and they have feasts of honey, and we call them " Flowers."

In a certain sense, therefore, you see the Botanical lecturer was quite right. There are no such things as Flowers—there are only Leaves. Nay, farther than this, there may be a dignity in the less happy, but unwithering leaf, which is, in some sort, better than the brief lily of its bloom ;—which the great poets always knew,—well ;— Chaucer, before Goethe ; and the writer of the first Psalm, before Chaucer. The Botanical lecturer was, in a deeper sense than he knew, right.

But in the deepest sense of all, the Botanical lecturer

was, to the extremity of wrongness, wrong ; for leaf, and root, and fruit, exist, all of them, only—that there may be flowers.   He disregarded the life and passion of the creature, which were its essence.   Had he looked for these, he would have recognized that in the thought of Nature herself, there is, in a plant, nothing else but its flowers.

Now in exactly the sense that modern Science declares there is no such thing as a Flower, it has declared there is no such thing as a Man, but only a transitional form of Ascidians and apes.   It may, or may not be true—it is not of the smallest consequence whether it be or not.   The real fact is, that, seen with human eyes, there is nothing else but man ; that all animals and beings beside him are only made that they may change into him ; that the world truly exists only in the presence of Man, acts only in the passion of Man.   The essence of light is in his eyes,—the centre of Force in his soul, —the pertinence of action in his deeds.

And all true science—which my Savoyard guide rightly scorned me when he thought I had not,—all true science is " savoir vivre."   But all your modern science is the contrary of that.   It is " savoir mourir."

And of its very discoveries, such as they are, it cannot make use.

That telegraphic signalling was a discovery ; and conceivably, some day, may be a useful one.   And there was some excuse for your being a little proud when, about

last sixth of April (Cœur de Lion's death-day, and
Albert Durer's), you knotted a copper wire all the way to
Bombay, and flashed a message along it, and back.

But what was the message, and what the answer?
Is India the better for what you said to her? Are you
the better for what she replied?

If not, you have only wasted an all-round-the-world's
length of copper wire,—which is, indeed, about the sum of
your doing. If you had had, perchance, two words of
common sense to say, though you had taken wearisome
time and trouble to send them ;—though you had written
them slowly in gold, and sealed them with a hundred
seals, and sent a squadron of ships of the line to carry
the scroll, and the squadron had fought its way round
the Cape of Good Hope, through a year of storms, with
loss of all its ships but one,—the two words of common
sense would have been worth the carriage, and more.
But you have not anything like so much as that to say,
either to India, or to any other place.

You think it a great triumph to make the sun draw
brown landscapes for you. That was also a discovery,
and some day may be useful. But the sun had drawn
landscapes before for you, not in brown, but in green, and
blue, and all imaginable colours, here in England. Not
one of you ever looked at them then ; not one of you
cares for the loss of them now, when you have shut the
sun out with smoke, so that he can draw nothing more,
except brown blots through a hole in a box. There was

a rocky valley between Buxton and Bakewell, once upon a time, divine as the Vale of Tempe; you might have seen the Gods there morning and evening—Apollo and all the sweet Muses of the light—walking in fair procession on the lawns of it, and to and fro· among the pinnacles of its crags. You cared neither for Gods nor grass, but for cash (which you did not know the way to get); you thought you could get it by what the *Times* calls "Railroad Enterprise." You Enterprised a Railroad through the valley—you blasted its rocks away, heaped thousands of tons of shale into its lovely stream. The valley is gone, and the Gods with it; and now, every fool in Buxton can be at Bakewell in half an hour, and every fool in Bakewell at Buxton; which you think a lucrative process of exchange—you Fools Everywhere.

To talk at a distance, when you have nothing to say, though you were ever so near; to go fast from this place to that, with nothing to do either at one or the other : these are powers certainly. Much more, power of increased Production, if you, indeed, had got it, would be something to boast of. But are you so entirely sure that you *have* got it—that the mortal disease of plenty, and afflictive affluence of good things, are all you have to dread ?

Observe. A man and a woman, with their children, properly trained, are able easily to cultivate as much ground as will feed them; to build as much wall and roof as will lodge them, and to build and weave as much cloth as will clothe them. They can all be perfectly

happy and healthy in doing this. Supposing that they
invent machinery which will build, plough, thresh, cook,
and weave, and that they have none of these things any
more to do, but may read, or play croquet, or cricket, all
day long, I believe myself that they will neither be so
good nor so happy as without the machines. But I waive
my belief in this matter for the time. I will assume that
they become more refined and moral persons, and that
idleness is in future to be the mother of all good. But
observe, I repeat, the power of your machine is only in
enabling them to be idle. It will not enable them to live
better than they did before, nor to live in greater numbers.
Get your heads quite clear on this matter. Out of so
much ground, only so much living is to be got, with or
without machinery. You may set a million of steam-
ploughs to work on an acre, if you like—out of that acre
only a given number of grains of corn will grow, scratch
or scorch it as you will. So that the question is not at
all whether, by having more machines, more of you can
live. No machines will increase the possibilities of life.
They only increase the possibilities of idleness. Suppose,
for instance, you could get the oxen in your plough driven
by a goblin, who would ask for no pay, not even a cream
bowl,—(you have nearly managed to get it driven by an
iron goblin, as it is ;)—Well, your furrow will take no more
seeds than if you had held the stilts yourself. But, instead
of holding them, you sit, I presume, on a bank beside the
field, under an eglantine ;—watch the goblin at his work,

and read poetry. Meantime, your wife in the house has also got a goblin to weave and wash for her. And she is lying on the sofa reading poetry.

Now, as I said, I don't believe you would be happier so, but I am willing to believe it; only, since you are already such brave mechanists, show me at least one or two places where you *are* happier. Let me see one small example of approach to this seraphic condition. *I* can show *you* examples, millions of them, of happy people, made happy by their own industry. Farm after farm I can show you, in Bavaria, Switzerland, the Tyrol, and such other places, where men and women are perfectly happy and good, without any iron servants. Show me, therefore, some English family, with its fiery familiar, happier than these. Or bring me,—for I am not inconvincible by any kind of evidence,—bring me the testimony of an English family or two to their increased felicity. Or if you cannot do so much as that, can you convince even themselves of it? They *are* perhaps happy, if only they knew how happy they were; Virgil thought so, long ago, of simple rustics; but you hear at present your steam-propelled rustics are crying out that they are anything else than happy, and that they regard their boasted 'progress "in the light of a monstrous Sham." I must tell you one little thing, however, which greatly perplexes my imagination of the relieved ploughman sitting under his rose bower, reading poetry. I have told it you before indeed, but I forget where. There was really

a great festivity, and expression of satisfaction in the
new order of things, down in Cumberland, a little while
ago ; some first of May, I think it was, a country festival,
such as the old heathens, who had no iron servants,
used to keep with piping and dancing. So I thought,
from the liberated country people—their work all done
for them by goblins—we should have some extraordinary
piping and dancing. But there was no dancing at all,
and they could not even provide their own piping. They
had their goblin to pipe for them. They walked in
procession after their steam plough, and their steam
plough whistled to them occasionally in the most melo-
dious manner it could. Which seemed to me, indeed, a
return to more than Arcadian simplicity ; for in old
Arcadia, ploughboys truly whistled as they went, for
want of thought ; whereas, here was verily a large company walking without thought, but not having any more
even the capacity of doing their own whistling.

But next, as to the inside of the house. Before you
got your power-looms, a woman could always make herself a chemise and petticoat of bright and pretty appearance. I have seen a Bavarian peasant-woman at church
in Munich, looking a much grander creature, and more
beautifully dressed, than any of the crossed and em-
broidered angels in Hesse's high-art frescoes ; (which
happened to be just above her, so that I could look
from one to the other). Well, here you are, in England,
served by household demons, with five hundred fingers,

at least, weaving, for one that used to weave in the day of Minerva. You ought to be able to show me five hundred dresses for one that used to be ; tidiness ought to have become five hundred-fold tidier ; tapestry should be increased into cinque-cento-fold iridescence of tapestry. Not only your peasant-girl ought to be lying on the sofa reading poetry, but she ought to have in her wardrobe five hundred petticoats instead of one. Is that, indeed, your issue ? or are you only on a curiously crooked way to it ?

It is just possible, indeed, that you may not have been allowed to get the use of the goblin's work—that other people may have got the use of it, and you none ; because, perhaps, you have not been able to evoke goblins wholly for your own personal service : but have been borrowing goblins from the capitalist, and paying interest, in the " position of William," on ghostly self-going planes; but suppose you had laid by capital enough, yourselves, to hire all the demons in the world,—nay,—all that are inside of it ; are you quite sure you know what you might best set them to work at ? and what " useful things " you should command them to make for you ? I told you, last month, that no economist going (whether by steam or ghost) knew what are useful things and what are not. Very few of you know, yourselves, except by bitter experience of the want of them. And no demons, either of iron or spirit, can ever make them.

There are three Material things, not only useful, but

essential to Life. No one "knows how to live" till he has got them.

These are, Pure Air, Water, and Earth.

There are three Immaterial things, not only useful, but essential to Life. No one knows how to live till he has got them.

These are, Admiration, Hope, and Love.*

Admiration—the power of discerning and taking delight in what is beautiful in visible Form, and lovely in human · Character ; and, necessarily, striving to produce what is beautiful in form, and to become what is lovely in character.

Hope—the recognition, by true Foresight, of better things to be reached hereafter, whether by ourselves or others ; necessarily issuing in the straightforward and undisappointable effort to advance, according to our proper power, the gaining of them.

Love, both of family and neighbour, faithful, and satisfied.

These are the six chiefly useful things to be got by Political Economy, when it *has* become a science. I will briefly tell you what modern Political Economy— the great "savoir mourir"—is doing with them.

The first three, I said, are Pure Air, Water, and Earth.

---

* Wordsworth, "Excursion," Book 4th ; in Moxon's edition, 1857 (stupidly without numbers to lines), vol. vi , p. 135.

Heaven gives you the main elements of these. You
can destroy them at your pleasure, or increase, almost
without limit, the available qualities of them.

You can vitiate the air by your manner of life, and of
death, to any extent. You might easily vitiate it so as
to bring such a pestilence on the globe as would end all
of you. You or your fellows, German and French, are
at present busy in vitiating it to the best of your power
in every direction ; chiefly at this moment with corpses,
and animal and vegetable ruin in war : changing men,
horses, and garden-stuff into noxious gas. But everywhere, and all day long, you are vitiating it with foul
chemical exhalations ; and the horrible nests, which you
call towns, are little more than laboratories for the distilla-
tion into heaven of venomous smokes and smells, mixed
with effluvia from decaying animal matter, and infectious
miasmata from purulent disease.

On the other hand, your power of purifying the
air, by dealing properly and swiftly with all substances
in corruption ; by absolutely forbidding noxious manufactures ; and by planting in all soils the trees which
cleanse and invigorate earth and atmosphere,—is literally
infinite. You might make every breath of air you draw,
food.

Secondly, your power over the rain and river-waters
of the earth is infinite. You can bring rain where
you will, by planting wisely and tending carefully ;—
drought where you will, by ravage of woods and neglect

of the soil. You might have the rivers of England as pure as the crystal of the rock; beautiful in falls, in lakes, in living pools; so full of fish that you might take them out with your hands instead of nets. Or you may do always as you have done now, turn every river of England into a common sewer, so that you cannot so much as baptize an English baby but with filth, unless you hold its face out in the rain; and even *that* falls dirty.

Then for the third, Earth,—meant to be nourishing for you, and blossoming. You have learned, about it, that there is no such thing as a flower; and as far as your scientific hands and scientific brains, inventive of explosive and deathful, instead of blossoming and life giving, Dust, can contrive, you have turned the Mother-Earth, Demeter,* into the Avenger-Earth, Tisiphone—

---

* Read this, for instance, concerning the Gardens of Paris :—one sentence in the letter is omitted; I will give it in full elsewhere, with its necessary comments :—

"*To the Editor of the Times.*

"*5th April,* 1871.

"SIR,—As the paragraph you quoted on Monday from the *Field* gives no idea of the destruction of the gardens round Paris, if you can spare me a very little space I will endeavour to supplement it.

"The public gardens in the interior of Paris, including the planting on the greater number of the Boulevards, are in a condition perfectly surprising when one considers the sufferings even well-to-do persons had to endure for want of fuel during the siege. Some of them, like the little oases in the centre of the Louvre, even look as pretty as ever. After a similar ordeal it is probable we should not have a stick left in London, and the presence of the very handsome planes on the Boulevards, and large trees in the various squares and gardens, after the winter of 1870—71, is most creditable to the population. But when one goes beyond the Champs Elysées and towards the Bois, down the once beautiful Avenue de l'Impératrice, a sad scene of desolation presents with the voice of your brother's blood crying out of it, in one wild harmony round all its murderous sphere.

This is what you have done for the three Material Useful Things.

---

itself. A year ago it was the finest avenue garden in existence; now a considerable part of the surface where troops were camped is about as filthy and as cheerless as Leicester Square or a sparsely furnished rubbish yard.

"The view into the once richly-wooded Bois from the huge and ugly banks of earth which now cross the noble roads leading into it is desolate indeed, the stump of the trees cut down over a large extent of its surface reminding one of the dreary scenes observable in many parts of Canada and the United States, where the stumps of the burnt or cut-down pines are allowed to rot away for years. The zone of the ruins round the vast belt of fortifications I need not speak of, nor of the other zone of destruction round each of the forts, as here houses and gardens and all have disappeared. But the destruction in the wide zone occupied by French and Prussian outposts is beyond description. I got to Paris the morning after the shooting of Generals Clement Thomas and Lecomte, and in consequence did not see so much of it as I otherwise might have done; but round the villages of Sceaux, Bourg-la-Reine, L'Hay, Vitry, and Villejuif, I saw an amount of havoc which the subscriptions to the French Horticultural Relief Fund will go but a very small way to repair. Notwithstanding all his revolutions and wars, the Frenchman usually found time to cultivate a few fruit trees, and the neighbourhood of the villages above mentioned was only a few of many covered by nurseries of young trees. When I last visited Vitry, in the autumn of 1868, the fields and hill-sides around were everywhere covered with trees; now the view across them is only interrupted by stumps about a foot high. When at Vitry on the 28th of March, I found the once fine nursery of M. Honoré Dufresne deserted, and many acres once covered with large stock and specimens cleared to the ground. And so it was in numerous other cases. It may give some notion of the effect of the war on the gardens and nurseries around Paris, when I state that, according to returns made up just before my visit to Vitry and Villejuif, it was found that around these two villages alone 2,400,400 fruit and other trees were destroyed. As to the private gardens, I cannot give a better idea of them than by describing the materials composing the protecting bank of a battery near Sceaux. It was made up of mattresses, sofas, and almost every other large article of furniture, with the earth stowed between. There were, in addition, nearly forty orange and oleander tubs gathered from the little gardens in the neighbourhood visible in various parts

Then for the Three Immaterial Useful Things. For Admiration, you have learnt contempt and conceit. There is no lovely thing ever yet done by man that you care for, or can understand ; but you are persuaded you are able to do much finer things yourselves. You gather, and exhibit together, as if equally instructive, what is infinitely bad, with what is infinitely good. You do not know which is which ; you instinctively prefer the Bad, and do more of it. You instinctively hate the Good, and destroy it.*

Then, secondly, for Hope. You have not so much spirit of it in you as to begin any plan which will not pay for ten years ; nor so much intelligence of it in you, (either politicians or workmen), as to be able to form one clear idea of what you would like your country to become.

---

of this ugly bank. One nurseryman at Sceaux, M. Keteleer, lost 1,500 vols. of books, which were not taken to Germany, but simply mutilated and thrown out of doors to rot. . . . Multiply these few instances by the number of districts occupied by the belligerents during the war, and some idea of the effects of glory on gardening in France may be obtained.

"W. ROBINSON."

* Last night (I am writing this on the 18th of April) I got a letter from Venice, bringing me the, I believe, too well-grounded, report that the Venetians have requested permission from the government of Italy to pull down their Ducal Palace, and "rebuild" it. Put up a horrible model of it, in its place, that is to say, for which their architects may charge a commission. Meantime, all their canals are choked with human dung, which they are too poor to cart away, but throw out at their windows.

And all the great thirteenth-century cathedrals in France have been destroyed, within my own memory, only that architects might charge commission for putting up false models of them in their place.

Then, thirdly, for Love. You were ordered by the Founder of your religion . to love your neighbour as yourselves.

You have founded an entire Science of Political Economy, on what you have stated to be the constant instinct of man —the desire to defraud his neighbour.

And you have driven your women mad, so that they ask no more for Love, nor for fellowship with you ; but stand against you, and ask for " justice."

Are there any of you who are tired of all this ? Any of you, Landlords or Tenants ? Employers or Workmen ?

Are there any landlords,—any masters,—who would like better to be served by men than by iron devils ?

Any tenants, any workmen, who can be true to their leaders and to each other ? who can vow to work and to live faithfully, for the sake of the joy of their homes ?

Will any such give the tenth of what they have, and of what they earn,—not to emigrate with, but to stay in England with ; and do what is in their hands and hearts to make her a happy England ?

I am not rich, (as people now estimate riches,) and great part of what I have is already engaged in maintaining art-workmen, or for other objects more or less of public utility. The tenth of whatever is left to me, estimated as accurately as I can, (you shall see the accounts,) I will make over to you in perpetuity, with the best security that English law can give, on Christmas Day of this year, with engagement to add the tithe of

whatever I earn afterwards.   Who else will help, with little
or much ? the object of such fund being, to begin, and
gradually—no matter how slowly—to increase, the buying
and securing of land in England, which shall not be
built upon, but cultivated by Englishmen, with their own
hands, and such help of force as they can find in wind
and wave.

I do not care with how many, or how few, this thing
is begun, nor on what inconsiderable scale,—if it be but
in two or three poor men's gardens.   So much, at least,
I can buy, myself, and give them.   If no help come,
I have done and said what I could, and there will be
an end.   If any help come to me, it is to be on the
following conditions :—We will try to take some small
piece of English ground, beautiful, peaceful, and fruitful.
We will have no steam-engines upon it, and no railroads ; we will have no untended or unthought-of creatures on it ; none wretched, but the sick ; none idle
but the dead.   We will have no liberty upon it ; but
instant obedience to known law, and appointed persons :
no equality upon it ; but recognition of every betterness
that we can find, and reprobation of every worseness.
When we want to go anywhere, we will go there
quietly and safely, not at forty miles an hour in the risk
of our lives ; when we want to carry anything anywhere,
we will carry it either on the backs of beasts, or on our
own, or in carts, or boats ; we will have plenty of flowers
and vegetables in our gardens, plenty of corn and grass

in our fields,—and few bricks. We will have some music and poetry ; the children shall learn to dance to it and sing it ;—perhaps some of the old people, in time, may also. We will have some art, moreover ; we will at least try if, like the Greeks, we can't make some pots. The Greeks used to paint pictures of gods on their pots ; we probably, cannot do as much, but we may put some pictures of insects on them, and reptiles ;—butterflies, and frogs, if nothing better. There was an excellent old potter in France who used to put frogs and vipers into his dishes, to the admiration of mankind ; we can surely put something nicer than that. Little by little, some higher art and imagination may manifest themselves among us ; and feeble rays of science may dawn for us. Botany, though too dull to dispute the existence of flowers ; and history, though too simple to question the nativity of men ;—nay—even perhaps an uncalculating and un-covetous wisdom, as of rude Magi, presenting, at such nativity, gifts of gold and frankincense.

Faithfully yours,

JOHN RUSKIN.

FORS CLAVIGERA.

LETTER THE 6th.

ELYSIAN FIELDS.

DENMARK HILL,
1st June, 1871.*

MY FRIENDS,

The main purpose of these letters having been stated in the last of them, it is needful that I should tell you why I approach the discussion of it in this so desultory way, writing (as it is too true that I must continue to write,) " of things that you little care for, in words that you cannot easily understand."

I write of things you care little for, knowing that what

---

* I think it best to publish this letter as it was prepared for press on the morning of the 25th of last month, at Abingdon, before the papers of that day had reached me. You may misinterpret its tone, and think it is written without feeling ; but I will endeavour to give you, in my next letter, a brief statement of the meaning, to the French and to all other nations, of this war, and its results : in the meantime, trust me, there is probably no other man living to whom, in the abstract, and irrespective of loss of family and property, the ruin of Paris is so great a sorrow as it is to me.

you least care for is, at this juncture, of the greatest
moment to you.

And I write in words you are little likely to understand, because I have no wish (rather the contrary) to
tell you anything that you can understand without taking
trouble. You usually read so fast that you can catch
nothing but the echo of your own opinions, which, of
course, you are pleased to see in print. I neither wish
to please, nor displease you ; but to provoke you to
think ; to lead you to think accurately ; and help you
to form, perhaps, some different opinions from those
you have now.

Therefore, I choose that you shall pay me the price
of two pots of beer, twelve times in the year, for my
advice, each of you who wants it. If you like to think
of me as a quack doctor, you are welcome ; and you
may consider the large margins, and thick paper, and
ugly pictures of my book, as my caravan, drum, and
skeleton. You would probably, if invited in that manner,
buy my pills ; and I should make a great deal of
money out of you ; but being an honest doctor, I still
mean you to pay me what you ought. You fancy, doubtless, that I write—as most other political writers do—
my 'opinions' ; and that one man's opinion is as good
as another's. You are much mistaken. When I only
opine things, I hold my tongue ; and work till I more
than opine—until I know them. If the things prove
unknowable, I, with final perseverance, hold my tongue

about them, and recommend a like practice to other
people. If the things prove knowable, as soon as I
know them, I am ready to write about them, if need
be ; not till then. That is what people call my 'arro-
gance.' They write and talk themselves, habitually, of
what they know nothing about ; they cannot in anywise
conceive the state of mind of a person who will not speak
till he knows ; and then tells them, serenely, " This is so ;
you may find it out for yourselves, if you choose ; but,
however little you may choose it, the thing is still so."

Now it has cost me twenty years of thought, and of
hard reading, to learn what I have to tell you in these
pamphlets ; and you will find, if you choose to find, it is
true ; and may prove, if you choose to prove, that it is
useful : and I am not in the least minded to compete for
your audience with the ' opinions ' in your damp journals,
morning and evening, the black of them coming off on
your fingers, and—beyond all washing—into your brains.
It is no affair of mine whether you attend to me or not ;
but yours wholly ; my hand is weary of pen-holding—my
heart is sick of thinking ; for my own part, I would not
write you these pamphlets though you would give me a
barrel of beer, instead of two pints, for them :—I write
them wholly for your sake ; I choose that you shall have
them decently printed on cream-coloured paper, and with
a margin underneath, which you can write on, if you like.
That is also for your sake : it is a proper form of book for
any man to have who can keep his books clean ; and if he

cannot, he has no business with books at all. It costs
me ten pounds to print a thousand copies, and five more
to give you a picture ; and a penny off my sevenpence to
send you the book ;—a thousand sixpences are twenty-five
pounds ; when you have bought a thousand Fors of me, I
shall therefore have five pounds for my trouble—and my
single shopman, Mr. Allen, five pounds for his ; we won't
work for less, either of us ; not that we would not, were it
good for you ; but it would be by no means good. And I
mean to sell all my large books, henceforward, in the same
way ; well printed, well bound, and at a fixed price ; and
the trade may charge a proper and acknowledged profit
for their trouble in retailing the book. Then the public
will know what they are about, and so will tradesmen ;
I, the first producer, answer, to the best of my power, for
the quality of the book ;—paper, binding, eloquence, and
all : the retail dealer charges what he ought to charge,
openly ; and if the public do not choose to give it, they
can't get the book. That is what I call legitimate business.
Then as for this misunderstanding of me—remember that
it is really not easy to understand anything, which you
have not heard before, if it relates to a complex subject ;
also, it is quite easy to misunderstand things that you are
hearing every day—which seem to you of the intelligiblest
sort. But I *can* only write of things in my own way and
as they come into my head ; and of the things I care for,
whether you care for them or not, as yet. I will answer
for it, you must care for some of them, in time.

To take an instance close to my hand : you would of course think it little conducive to your interests that I should give you any account of the wild hyacinths which are opening in flakes of blue fire, this day, within a couple of miles of me, in the glades of Bagley wood through which the Empress Maud fled in the snow, (and which, by the way, I slink through, myself, in some discomfort, lest the gamekeeper of the college of the gracious Apostle St. John should catch sight of me ; not that he would ultimately decline to make a distinction between a poacher and a professor, but that I dislike the trouble of giving an account of myself). Or, if even you would bear with a scientific sentence or two about them, explaining to you that they were only green leaves turned blue, and that it was of no consequence whether they were either ; and that, as flowers, they were scientifically to be considered as not in existence,—you will, I fear, throw my letter, even though it has cost you seven-pence, aside at once, when I remark to you that these wood hyacinths of Bagley have something to do with the battle of Marathon, and if you knew it, are of more vital interest to you than even the Match Tax.

Nevertheless, as I shall feel it my duty, some day, to speak to you of Theseus and his vegetable soup, so, to-day, I think it necessary to tell you that the wood-hyacinth is the best English representative of the tribe of flowers which the Greeks called " Asphodel," and which they thought the heroes who had fallen in the battle of Marathon, or in any other battle, fought in just quarrel, were to be rewarded, and enough rewarded, by living in fields-full of ; fields called, by them, Elysian, or the Fields of Coming, as you and I talk of the good time 'Coming,' though with perhaps different views as to the nature of the to be expected goodness.

Now what the Chancellor of the Exchequer said the other day to the Civil Engineers (see Saturday Review, April 29th,) is entirely true ; namely, that in any of our colliery or cartridge-manufactory explosions, we send as many men (or women) into Elysium as were likely to get there after the battle of Marathon ;* and that is, indeed, like the rest of our economic arrangements, very fine, and pleasant to think upon ; neither may it be doubted, on modern principles of religion and equality, that every collier and cartridge-filler is as fit for Elysium as any heathen could be ; and that in all these respects the battle of Marathon is no more deserving of English notice. But what I want you to reflect upon, as of moment to you, is whether you *really* care for the hyacinthine Elysium you are going to ? and if you do, why you should not live a little while in Elysium here, instead of waiting so patiently, and working so hardly, to be blown or flattened into it ? The hyacinths will grow well enough on the top of the ground, if you will leave

---

* Of course this was written, and in type, before the late catastrophe in Paris ; and the one at Dunkirk is, I suppose, long since forgotten, much more our own good beginning at—Birmingham—was it ? I forget, myself, now.

off digging away the bottom of it ; and another plant of
the asphodel species, which the Greeks thought of more
importance even than hyacinths—onions ; though, indeed,
one dead hero is represented by Lucian as finding something to complain of even in Elysium, because he got
nothing but onions there to eat. But it is simply, I
assure you, because the French did not understand
that hyacinths and onions were the principal things to
fill their existing Elysian Fields, or Champs Elysées,
with, but chose to have carriages, and roundabouts,
instead, that a tax on matches in those fields would
be, nowadays, so much more productive than one on
Asphodel ; and I see that only a day or two since
even a poor Punch's show could not play out its play
in Elysian peace, but had its corner knocked off by a
shell from Mont Valérien, and the dog Toby " seriously
alarmed."

One more instance of the things you don't care for,
that are vital to you, may be better told now than
hereafter.

In my plan for our practical work, in last number, you
remember I said, we must try and make some pottery,
and have some music, and that we would have no steam
engines. On this I received a singular letter from a
resident at Birmingham, advising me that the colours for
my pottery must be ground by steam, and my musical
instruments constructed by it. To this, as my correspondent was an educated person, and knew Latin, I

ventured to answer that porcelain had been painted before
the time of James Watt; that even music was not entirely
a recent invention ; that my poor company, I feared,
would deserve no better colours than Apelles and Titian
made shift with, or even the Chinese ; and that I could
not find any notice of musical instruments in the time of
David, for instance, having been made by steam.

To this my correspondent again replied that he supposed David's " twangling upon the harp " would have
been unsatisfactory to modern taste ; in which sentiment
I concurred with him, (thinking of the Cumberland procession, without dancing, after its sacred, cylindrical Ark).
We shall have to be content, however, for our part, with
a little " twangling " on such roughly-made harps, or even
shells, as the Jews and Greeks got their melody out of,
though it must indeed be little conceivable in a modern
manufacturing town that a nation could ever have existed
which imaginarily dined on onions in Heaven, and made
harps of the near relations of turtles on Earth. But
to keep to our crockery, you know I told you that for
some time we should not be able to put any pictures of
Gods on it ; and you might think that would be of small
consequence : but it is of moment that we should at least
try—for indeed that old French potter, Palissy, was nearly
the last of potters in France, or England either, who could
have done so, if anybody had wanted Gods.   But nobody
in his time did ;—they only wanted Goddesses, of a demi-
divine-monde pattern ; Palissy, not well able to produce

such, took to moulding innocent frogs and vipers instead, in his dishes ; but at Sèvres and other places for shaping of courtly clay, the charmingest things were done, as you probably saw at the great peace-promoting Exhibition of 1851 ; and not only the first rough potter's fields, tileries, as they called them, or Tuileries, but the little den where Palissy long after worked under the Louvre, were effaced and forgotten in the glory of the House of France ; until the House of France forgot also that to it, no less than the House of Israel, the words were spoken, not by a painted God, " As the clay is in the hands of the potter, so are ye in mine ; " and thus the stained and vitrified show of it lasted, as you have seen, until the Tuileries again became the Potter's field, to bury, not strangers in, but their own souls, no more ashamed of Traitorhood, but invoking Traitorhood, as if it covered, instead of constituting, uttermost shame ;—until, of the kingdom and its glory there is not a shard left, to take fire out of the hearth.

Left—to men's eyes, I should have written. To their thoughts, is left yet much ; for true kingdoms and true glories cannot pass away. What France has had of such, remain to her. What any of us can find of such, will remain to us. Will you look back, for an instant, again to the end of my last Letter, p. 23, and consider the state of life described there :—" No liberty, but instant obedience to known law and appointed persons ; no equality, but recognition of every betterness and reprobation of every worseness; and none idle but the dead."

I beg you to observe that last condition especially. You will debate for many a day to come the causes that have brought this misery upon France, and there are many; but one is chief—chief cause, now and always, of evil everywhere; and I see it at this moment, in its deadliest form, out of the window of my quiet English inn. It is the 21st of May, and a bright morning, and the sun shines, for once, warmly on the wall opposite, a low one, of ornamental pattern, imitative in brick of wood-work (as if it had been of wood-work, it would, doubtless, have been painted to look like brick). Against this low decorative edifice leans a ruddy-faced English boy of seventeen or eighteen, in a white blouse and brown corduroy trousers, and a domical felt hat; with the sun, as much as can get under the rim, on his face, and his hands in his pockets; listlessly watching two dogs at play. He is a good boy, evidently, and does not care to turn the play into a fight; * still it is not interesting enough to him, as play, to relieve the extreme distress of his idleness, and he occasionally takes his hands out of his pockets, and claps them at the dogs, to startle them.

The ornamental wall he leans against surrounds the county police-office, and the residence at the end of it,

---

* This was at seven in the morning; he had them fighting at half-past

appropriately called "Gaol Lodge." This county gaol, police-office, and a large gasometer, have been built by the good people of Abingdon to adorn the principal entrance to their town from the south. It was once quite one of the loveliest, as well as historically inte-resting, scenes in England. A few cottages and their gardens, sloping down to the river-side, are still left, and an arch or two of the great monastery; but the principal object from the road is now the gaol, and from the river the gasometer. It is curious that since the English have believed (as you will find the editor of the Liverpool Daily Post, quoting to you from Macaulay, in his leader of the 9th of this month), "the only cure for Liberty is more liberty," (which is true enough, for when you have got all you can, you will be past physic,) they always make their gaols conspicuous and ornamental. Now I have no objec-tion, myself, detesting, as I do, every approach to liberty, to a distinct manifestation of gaol, in proper quarters; nay, in the highest, and in the close neighbourhood of palaces; perhaps, even, with a convenient passage, and Ponte de' Sospiri, from one to the other, or, at least, a pleasant access by water-gate and down the river; but I do not see why in these days of 'incurable' liberty, the prospect in approaching a quiet English county town should be a gaol, and nothing else.

That being so, however, the country boy, in his white blouse, leans placidly against the prison wall this bright Sunday morning, little thinking what a luminous sign-post he is making of himself, and living gnomon of sun-dial, of which the shadow points sharply to the subtlest cause of the fall of France, and of England, as is too likely, after her.

Your hands in your own pockets, in the morning. That is the beginning of the last day ; your hands in other people's pockets at noon ; that is the height of the last day ; and the gaol, ornamented or otherwise (assuredly the great gaol of the grave), for the night. That is the history of nations under judgment. Don't think I say this to any single class ; least of all specially to you ; the rich are continually, nowadays, reproaching you with your wish to be idle. It is very wrong of you ; but, do they want to work all day, themselves ? All mouths are very properly open now against the Paris Communists because they fight that they may get wages for marching about with flags. What do the upper classes fight for, then ? What have they fought for since the world became upper and lower, but that they also might have wages for walking about with flags, and that mischievously ? It is very wrong of the Communists to steal church-plate and candlesticks. Very wrong indeed ; and much good may they get of their pawnbrokers' tickets. Have you any notion (I mean that you shall have some soon) how much the fathers and fathers' fathers of these men, for a thousand years back, have paid their priests, to keep them in plate and candlesticks ? You need not think I am a republican, or that I like to see priests ill-treated, and their candlesticks carried off. I have many friends among priests, and should have had more had I not long been trying to make them see that they have long trusted too much in candlesticks, not quite enough in candles ; not at all enough in the sun, and least of all enough in the sun's Maker. Scientific people indeed of late opine the sun to have been produced by collision, and to be a splendidly permanent railroad accident, or explosive Elysium : also I noticed, only yesterday, that gravitation itself is announced to the members of the Royal Institution as the result of vibratory motion. Some day, perhaps, the members of the Royal Institution will proceed to inquire after the cause of—vibratory motion. Be that as it may, the Beginning, or Prince of Vibration, as modern science has it,—Prince of Peace, as old science had it,— continues through all scientific analysis, His own arrangements about the sun, as also about other lights, lately hidden or burning low. And these are primarily, that He has appointed a great power to rise and set in heaven, which gives life, and warmth, and motion, to the bodies of men, and beasts, creeping things, and flowers ; and which also causes light and colour in the eyes of things that have eyes. And He has set above the souls of men, on earth, a great law or Sun of Justice or Righteousness, which brings also life and health in the daily strength and spreading of it, being spoken of in the priest's language, (which they never explain to anybody, and now wonder that nobody understands,) as having " healing in its wings : " and the obedience to this law, as it gives strength to the heart, so it gives light to the eyes of souls that have got any eyes, so that they begin to see each other as lovely, and to love each other.   That is the final law respecting the sun, and all manner of minor lights and candles, down to rushlights ; and I once got it fairly explained, two years ago, to an intelligent and obliging wax-and-tallow chandler at Abbeville, in whose shop I used to sit sketching in rainy days ; and watching the cartloads of ornamental candles which he used to supply for the church at the far east end of the town, (I forget what saint it belongs to, but it is opposite the late Emperor's large new cavalry barracks,) where the young ladies of the better class in Abbeville had just got up a beautiful evening service, with a pyramid of candles which it took at least half an hour to light, and as long to put out again, and which, when lighted up to the top of the church, were only to be looked at themselves, and sung to, and not to light anybody or anything.   I got the tallow-chandler to calculate vaguely the probable cost of the candles lighted in this manner, every day, in all the churches of France ; and then I asked him how many cottagers' wives he knew round Abbeville itself who could afford, without pinching, either dip or mould in the evening to make their children's clothes by, and whether, if the pink and green beeswax of the district were divided every afternoon among them, it might not be quite as honourable to God, and as good for the candle trade ?

Which he admitted readily enough ; but what I should have tried to convince the young ladies themselves of, at the evening service, would probably not have been admitted so readily ; —that they themselves were nothing more than an extremely graceful kind of wax-tapers which had got into their heads that they were only to be looked at, for the honour of God, and not to light anybody.

Which is indeed too much the notion of even the masculine aristocracy of Europe at this day. One can imagine them, indeed, modest in the matter of their own luminousness, and more timid of the tax on agri-cultural horses and carts, than of that on lucifers ; but it would be well if they were content, here in Eng-land, however dimly phosphorescent themselves, to bask in the sunshine of May at the end of Westminster Bridge, (as my boy on Abingdon Bridge,) with their backs against the large edifice they have built there,— an edifice, by the way, to my own poor judgment, less contributing to the adornment of London, than the new police-office to that of Abingdon. But the English squire, after his fashion, sends himself to that highly decorated gaol all spring-time ; and cannot be content with his hands in his own pockets, nor even in yours and mine ; but claps and laughs, semi-idiot that he is, at dog-fights on the floor of the House, which, if he knew it, are indeed dog-fights of the Stars in their courses, Sirius against Procyon ; and of the havock and loosed dogs of war, makes, as the Times correspondent says they make, at Versailles, of the siege of Paris, " the Entertainment of the Hour."

You think that, perhaps, an unjust saying of him, as he will, assuredly, himself. He would fain put an end to this wild work, if he could, he thinks.

My friends, I tell you solemnly, the sin of it all, down to this last night's doing, or undoing, (for it is Monday now, I waited before finishing my letter, to see if the Sainte Chapelle would follow the Vendome Column ;) the sin of it, I tell you, is not that poor rabble's, spade and pickaxe in hand among the dead ; nor yet the blasphemer's, making noise like a dog by the defiled altars of our Lady of Victories ; and round the barricades, and the ruins, of the Street of Peace.

This cruelty has been done by the kindest of us, and the most honourable ; by the delicate women, by the nobly-nurtured men, who through their happy and, as they thought, holy lives, have sought, and still seek, only " the entertainment of the hour." And this robbery has been taught to the hands,—this blasphemy to the lips,—of the lost poor, by the False Prophets who have taken the name of Christ in vain, and leagued themselves with His chief enemy, " Covetousness, which is idolatry."

Covetousness, lady of Competition and of deadly Care ; idol above the altars of Ignoble Victory ; builder of streets, in cities of Ignoble Peace. I have given you the picture of her—your goddess and only Hope—as

Giotto saw her : dominant in prosperous Italy as in prosperous England, and having her hands clawed then, as now, so that she can only clutch, not work ; also you shall read next month with me what one of Giotto's friends says of her—a rude versifier, one of the twangling harpers ; as Giotto was a poor painter for low price, and with colours ground by hand ; but such cheap work must serve our turn for this time ; also, here, is portrayed for you* one of the ministering angels of the

goddess ; for she herself, having ears set wide to the wind, is careful to have wind-instruments provided by her servants for other people's ears.

This servant of hers was drawn by the court portrait-

---

* Engraved, as also the woodcut in the April number, carefully after Holbein, by my coal-waggon-assisting assistant : but he has missed his mark somewhat, here ; the imp's abortive hands, hooked processes only, like Envy's, and pterodactylous, are scarcely seen in their clutch of the bellows, and there are other faults. We will do it better for you, afterwards.

painter, Holbein; and was a councillor at poor-law boards, in his day; counselling then, as some of us have, since, " Bread of Affliction and Water of Affliction" for the vagrant as such,—which is, indeed, good advice, if you are quite sure the vagrant has, or may have, a home; not otherwise. But we will talk further of this next month, taking into council one of Holbein's prosaic friends, as well as that singing friend of Giotto's—an English lawyer and country gentleman, living on his farm, at Chelsea (somewhere near Cheyne Row, I believe) —and not unfrequently visited there by the King of England, who would ask himself unexpectedly to dinner at the little Thames-side farm, though the floor of it was only strewn with green rushes. It was burnt at last, rushes, ricks, and all; some said because bread of affliction and water of affliction had been served to heretics there, its master being a stout Catholic; and, singularly enough, also a Communist; so that because of the fire, and other matters, the King at last ceased to dine at Chelsea. We will have some talk, however, with the farmer, ourselves, some day soon; meantime and always, believe me,

Faithfully yours,

JOHN RUSKIN.

POSTSCRIPT.

25th May (*early morning*).—Reuter's final telegram, in the Echo of last night, being " The Louvre and the Tuileries are in flames, the Federals having set fire to them with petroleum," it is interesting to observe how, in fulfilment of the Mechanical Glories of our age, its ingenious Gomorrah manufactures, and supplies to demand, her own brimstone ; achieving also a quite scientific, instead of miraculous, descent of it from Heaven ; and ascent of it, where required, without any need of cleaving or quaking of earth, except in a super-ficially ' vibratory ' manner.

Nor can it be less encouraging to you to see how, with a sufficiently curative quantity of Liberty, you may defend yourselves against all danger of over-production, especially in art ; but, in case you should ever wish to re-'produce' any of the combustibles (as oil, or canvas) used in these Parisian Economies, you will do well to inquire of the author of the " Essay on Liberty " whether he considers oil of linseed, or petroleum, as best fulfilling his definition, " utilities fixed and embodied in material objects."

FORS CLAVIGERA.

DENMARK HILL,
1st July, 1871.

MY FRIENDS,

IT seldom chances, my work lying chiefly among stones, clouds, and flowers, that I am brought into any freedom of intercourse with my fellow-creatures ; but since the fighting in Paris I have dined out several times, and spoken to the persons who sat next me, and to others when I went upstairs ; and done the best I could to find out what . people thought about the fighting, or thought they ought to think about it, or thought they ought to say. I had, of course, no hope of finding any one thinking what they ought to do. But I have not yet, a little to my surprise, met with any one who either appeared to be sadder, or professed himself wiser for anything that has happened.

It is true that I am neither sadder nor wiser,

because of it, myself. But then I was so sad before, that nothing could make me sadder ; and getting wiser has always been to me a very slow process,—(sometimes even quite stopping for whole days together),—so that if two or three new ideas fall in my way at once, it only puzzles me ; and the fighting in Paris has given me more than two or three.

The newest of all these new ones, and, in fact, quite a glistering and freshly minted idea to me, is the Parisian notion of Communism, as far as I understand it, (which I don't profess to do altogether, yet, or I should be wiser than I was, with a vengeance).

For, indeed, I am myself a Communist of the old school—reddest also of the red ; and was on the very point of saying so at the end of my last letter ; only the telegram about the Louvre's being on fire stopped me, because I thought the Communists of the new school, as I could not at all understand them, might not quite understand me. For we Communists of the old school think that our property belongs to everybody, and everybody's property to us ; so of course I thought the Louvre belonged to me as much as to the Parisians, and expected they would have sent word over to me, being an Art Professor, to ask whether I wanted it burnt down. But no message or intimation to that effect ever reached me.

Then the next bit of new coinage in the way of notion which I have picked up in Paris streets, is the present meaning of the French word 'Ouvrier,' which in my time the dictionaries used to give as 'Workman,' or 'Working-man.' For again, I have spent many days, not to say years, with the working-men of our English school myself; and I know that, with the more advanced of them, the gathering word is that which I gave you at the end of my second number—" To do good work, whether we live or die." Whereas I perceive the gathering, or rather scattering, word of the French 'ouvrier' is, 'To *undo* good work, whether we live or die.'

And this is the third, and the last, I will tell you for the present, of my new ideas, but a troublesome one: namely, that we are henceforward to have a duplicate power of political economy; and that the new Parisian expression for its first principle is not to be 'laissez faire,' but ' laissez *re*faire.'

I cannot, however, make anything of these new French fashions of thought till I have looked at them quietly a little ; so to-day I will content myself with telling you what we Communists of the old school meant by Communism ; and it will be worth your hearing, for—I tell you simply in my 'arrogant' way —we know, and have known, what Communism - is— for our fathers knew it, and told us, three thousand years ago ; while you baby Communists do not so much as know what the name means, in your own English or French—no, not so much as whether a House of

Commons implies, or does not imply, also a House
of Uncommons ; nor whether the Holiness of the
Commune, which Garibaldi came to fight for, had any
relation to the Holiness of the 'Communion' which he
came to fight against.

Will you be at the pains, now, however, to learn
rightly, and once for all, what Communism is? First,
it means that everybody must work in common, and do
common or simple work for his dinner ; and that if
any man will not do it, he must not have his dinner.
That much, perhaps, you thought you knew?—but
you did not think we Communists of the old school
knew it also? You shall have it, then, in the words
of the Chelsea farmer and stout Catholic, I was telling
you of, in last number. He was born in Milk
Street, London, three hundred and ninety-one years
ago, (1480, a year I have just been telling my Oxford
pupils to remember for manifold reasons,) and he
planned a Commune flowing with milk and honey,
and otherwise Elysian ; and called it the 'Place of
Wellbeing,' or Utopia ; which is a word you perhaps
have occasionally used before now, like others, without
understanding it ;—(in the article of the Liverpool
Daily Post before referred to, it occurs felicitously
seven times). You shall use it in that stupid way no
more, if I can help it. Listen how matters really are
managed there.

" The chief, and almost the only business of the

government,* is to take care that no man may live idle, but that every one may follow his trade diligently : yet they do not wear themselves out with perpetual toil from morning till night, as if they were beasts of burden, which, as it is indeed a heavy slavery, so it is everywhere the common course of life amongst all mechanics except the Utopians ; but they, dividing the day and night into twenty-four hours, appoint six of these for work, three of which are before dinner and three after ; they then sup, and, at eight o'clock, counting from noon, go to bed and sleep eight hours : the rest of their time, besides that taken up in work, eating, and sleeping, is left to every man's discretion ; yet they are not to abuse that interval to luxury and idleness, but must employ it in some proper exercise, according to their various inclinations, which is, for the most part, reading.

"But the time appointed for labour is to be narrowly examined, otherwise, you may imagine that, since there are only six hours appointed for work, they may fall under a scarcity of necessary provisions : but it is so far from being true that this time is not sufficient for supplying them with plenty of all things, either necessary or convenient, that it is rather too much ; and this you will easily apprehend, if you consider how great a

---

* I spare you, for once, a word for 'government' used by this old author, which would have been unintelligible to you, and is so, except in its general sense, to me, too.

part of all other nations is quite idle. First, women
generally do little, who are the half of mankind ; and,
if some few women are diligent, their husbands are
idle : then,— . . . . ."

What then ?

We will stop a minute, friends, if you please, for I
want you before you read what then, to be once more
made fully aware that this farmer who is speaking to
you is one of the sternest Roman Catholics of his stern
time ; and at the fall of Cardinal Wolsey, became Lord
High Chancellor of England in his stead.

"—then, consider the great company of idle priests, and
of those that are called religious men ; add to these, all
rich men, chiefly those that have estates in land, who
are called noblemen and gentlemen, together with their
families, made up of idle persons, that are kept more
for show·than use ; add to these, all those strong and
lusty beggars that go about, pretending some disease
in excuse for their begging ; and, upon the whole
account, you will find that the number of those by
whose labours mankind is supplied is much less than
you, perhaps, imagined : then, consider how few of
those that work are employed in labours that are of
real service! for we, who measure all things by money,
give rise to many trades that are both vain and
superfluous, and serve only to support riot and luxury :
for if those who work were employed only in such
things as the conveniences of life require, there would

be such an abundance of them, *that the prices of them would so sink that tradesmen could not be maintained by their gains;"*—(italics mine—Fair and softly, Sir Thomas! we must have a shop round the corner, and a pedlar or two on fair-days, yet;)—" if all those who labour about useless things were set to more profitable employments, and if all that languish out their lives in sloth and idleness (every one of whom consumes as much as any two of the men that are at work) were forced to labour, you may easily imagine that a small proportion of time would serve for doing all that is either necessary, profitable, or pleasant to mankind, especially while pleasure is kept within its due bounds: this appears very plainly in Utopia ; for there, in a great city, and in all the territory that lies round it, you can scarce find five hundred, either men or women, by their age and strength capable of labour, that are not engaged in it! even the heads of government, though excused by the law, yet do not excuse themselves, but work, that, by their examples, they may excite the industry of the rest of the people."

You see, therefore, that there is never any fear, among us of the old school, of being out of work ; but there is great fear, among many of us, lest we should not do the work set us well ; for, indeed, we thorough-going Communists make it a part of our daily duty to consider how common we are ; and how few of us have any brains or souls worth speaking of, or fit to trust to ;—that being the, alas, almost unexceptionable lot of human creatures. Not that we think ourselves, (still less, call ourselves without thinking so,) miserable sinners, for we are not in anywise miserable, but quite comfortable for the most part ; and we are not sinners, that we know of ; but are leading godly, righteous, and sober lives, to the best of our power, since last Sunday ; (on which day some of us were, we regret to be informed, drunk ;) but we are of course common creatures enough, the most of us, and thankful if we may be gathered up in St. Peter's sheet, so as not to be uncivilly or unjustly called unclean too. And therefore our chief concern is to find out any among us wiser and of better make than the rest, and to get them, if they will for any persuasion take the trouble, to rule over us, and teach us how to behave, and make the most of what little good is in us.

So much for the first law of old Communism, respecting work. Then the second respects property, and it is that the public, or common, wealth, shall be more and statelier in all its substance than private or singular wealth ; that is to say (to come to my own special business for a moment) that there shall be only cheap and few pictures, if any, in the insides of houses, where nobody but the owner can see them ; but costly pictures, and many, on the outsides of houses, where the people can see them : also that the Hôtel-de-Ville, or Hotel of the whole Town, for the transaction of its common business, shall be a magnificent building, much rejoiced in by the people, and with its tower seen far away through the clear air ; but that the hotels for private business or pleasure, cafés, taverns, and the like, shall be low, few, plain, and in back streets ; more especially such as furnish singular and uncommon drinks and refreshments ; but that the fountains which furnish the people's common drink shall be very lovely and stately, and adorned with precious marbles, and the like. Then farther, according to old Communism, the private dwellings of uncommon persons—dukes and lords—are to be very simple, and roughly put together,—such persons being supposed to be above all care for things that please the commonalty ; but the buildings for public or common service, more especially schools, almshouses, and workhouses, are to be externally of a majestic character, as being for noble purposes and charities ; and in their interiors furnished with many luxuries for the poor and sick. And, finally and chiefly, it is an absolute law of old Communism that the fortunes of private persons should be small, and of little account in the State ; but the common treasure of the whole nation should be of superb and precious things in redundant quantity, as pictures, statues, precious books ; gold and silver vessels, preserved from ancient times ; gold and silver bullion laid up for use, in case of any chance need of buying anything suddenly from foreign nations ; noble horses, cattle, and sheep, on the public lands ;

and vast spaces of land for culture, exercise, and garden, round the cities, full of flowers, which, being everybody's property, nobody could gather ; and of birds which, being everybody's property, nobody could shoot. And, in a word, that instead of a common poverty, or national debt, which every poor person in the nation is taxed annually to fulfil his part of, there should be a common wealth, or national reverse of debt, consisting of pleasant things, which every poor person in the nation should be summoned to receive his dole of, annually ; and of pretty things, which every person capable of admiration, foreigners as well as natives, should unfeignedly admire, in an æsthetic, and not a covetous manner (though for my own part I can't understand what it is that I am taxed now to defend, or what foreign nations are supposed to covet, here). But truly, a nation that has got anything to defend of real public interest, can usually hold it ; and a fat Latin communist gave for sign of the strength of his commonalty, in its strongest time,—

> " Privatus illis census erat brevis
> Commune magnum ; "

which you may get any of your boys or girls to translate for you, and remember ; remembering, also, that the commonalty or publicity depends for its goodness on the nature of the *thing* that is common, and that . is public. When the French cried, " Vive la République ! " after the battle of Sedan, they were thinking only of the

Publique, in the word, and not of the Re in it. But that is the essential part of it, for that " Re " is not like the mischievous Re in Reform, and Refaire, which the words had better be without ; but it is short for *res*, which means ' thing' ; and when you cry, " Live the Republic," the question is mainly, what thing it is you wish to be publicly alive, and whether you are striving for a Common-Wealth, and Public-Thing ; or, as too plainly in Paris, for a Common-Illth, and Public-Nothing, or even Public-Less-than-nothing and Common Deficit.

Now all these laws respecting public and private property, are accepted in the same terms by the entire body of us Communists of the old school ; but with respect to the management of both, we old Reds fall into two classes, differing, not indeed in colour of redness, but in depth of tint of it—one class being, as it were, only of a delicately pink, peach-blossom, or dog-rose redness ; but the other, to which I myself do partly, and desire wholly, to belong, as I told you, reddest of the red—that is to say, full crimson, or even dark crimson, passing into that deep colour of the blood which made the Spaniards call it blue, instead of red, and which the Greeks call φοινίκεος, being an intense phœnix or flamingo colour : and this not merely, as in the flamingo feathers, a colour on the outside, but going through and through, ruby-wise ; so that Dante, who is one of the few people who have ever beheld our queen full in the face, says of her that, if she had been in a fire, he could not have seen her at all, so fire-colour she was, all through.*

And between these two sects or shades of us, there is this difference in our way of holding our common faith, (that our neighbour's property is ours, and ours his,) namely, that the rose-red division of us are content in their diligence of care to preserve or guard from injury or loss their neighbours' property, as their own ; so that they may be called, not merely dog-rose red, but even 'watch-dog-rose' red ; being, indeed, more careful and anxious for the safety of the possessions of other people, (especially their masters,) than for any of their own ; and also more sorrowful for any wound or harm suffered by any creature in their sight, than for hurt to themselves. So that they are Communists, even less in their having part in all common well-being of their neighbours, than part in all common pain : being yet, on the whole, infinite gainers ; for there is in this world infinitely more joy than pain to be shared, if you will only take your share when it is set for you.

The vermilion, or Tyrian-red sect of us, however, are not content merely with this carefulness and watchfulness over our neighbours' good, but we cannot rest unless we are giving what we can spare of our own ; and the more precious it is, the more we want to divide

* "Tanto rossa, ch' appena fora dentro al fuoco nota.' —*Purg.*, xxix. 122.

it with somebody. So that above all things, in what we value most of possessions, pleasant sights, and true knowledge, we cannot relish seeing any pretty things unless other people see them also; neither can we be content to know anything for ourselves, but must contrive, somehow, to make it known to others.

And as thus especially we like to give knowledge away, so we like to have it good to give, (for, as for selling knowledge, thinking it comes by the spirit of Heaven, we hold the selling of it to be only a way of selling God again, and utterly Iscariot's business;) also, we know that the knowledge made up for sale is apt to be watered and dusted, or even itself good for nothing; and we try, for our part, to get it, and give it, pure: the mere fact that it is to be given away at once to anybody who asks to have it, and immediately wants to use it, is a continual check upon us. For instance, when Colonel North, in the House of Commons, on the 20th of last month, (as reported in the Times,) " would simply observe, in conclusion, that it was impossible to tell how many thousands of the young men who were to be embarked for India next September, would be marched, not to the hills, but to their graves ; " any of us Tyrian-reds " would simply observe " that the young men themselves ought to be constantly, and on principle, informed of their destination before embarking ; and that this pleasant communicativeness of what knowledge on the subject was to be got, would soon render quite possible the attainment of more. So also, in abstract science, the instant habit of making true discoveries common property, cures us of a bad trick which one may notice to have much hindered scientific persons lately, of rather spending their time in hiding their neighbours' discoveries, than improving their own: whereas, among us, scientific flamingoes are not only openly graced for discoveries, but openly disgraced for coveries ; and that sharply and permanently ; so that there is rarely a hint or thought among them of each other's being wrong, but quick confession of whatever is found out rightly.*

But the point in which we dark-red Communists differ most from other people is, that we dread, above all things, getting miserly of virtue ; and if there be any in us, or among us, we try forthwith to get it made common, and would fain hear the mob crying for some of that treasure, where it seems to have accumulated. I say, ' seems,' only : for though, at first, all the finest virtue looks as if it were laid up with the rich, (so that, generally, a millionaire would be much surprised at hearing that

---

* Confession always a little painful, however ; scientific envy being the most difficult of all to conquer. I find I did much injustice to the botanical lecturer, as well as to my friend. in my last letter ; and, indeed, suspected as much at the time ; but having some botanical notions myself, which I am vain of, I wanted the lecturer's to be wrong, and stopped cross-examining my friend as soon as I had got what suited me. Nevertheless, the general statement that follows, remember, rests on no tea-table chat ; and the tea-table chat itself is accurate, as far as it goes.

his daughter had made a *petroleuse* of herself, or that his
son had murdered anybody for the sake of their watch
and cravat),—it is not at all clear to us dark-reds that
this virtue, proportionate to income, is of the right sort ;
and we believe that even if it were, the people who keep
it thus all to themselves, and leave the so called *canaille*
without any, vitiate what they keep by keeping it, so
that it is like manna laid up through the night, which
breeds worms in the morning.

You see, also, that we dark-red Communists, since we
exist only in giving, must, on the contrary, hate with a
perfect hatred all manner of thieving : even to Cœur-de-
Lion's tar-and-feather extreme ; and of all thieving, we
d slike thieving on trust most, (so that, if we ever get to
be strong enough to do what we want, and chance to
catch hold of any failed bankers, their necks will not be
worth half an hour's purchase). So also, as we think
virtue diminishes in the honour and force of it in proportion to income, we think vice increases in the force
and shame of it, and is worse in kings and rich people
than in poor ; and worse on a large scale than on a
narrow one ; and worse when deliberate than hasty. So
that we can understand one man's coveting a piece of
vineyard-ground for a garden of herbs, and stoning the
master of it, (both of them being Jews ;)—and yet the
dogs ate queen's flesh for that, and licked king's blood !
but for two nations—both Christians—to covet their
neighbours' vineyards, all down beside the River of their

border, and slay until the River itself runs red! The little pool of Samaria!—shall all the snows of the Alps, or the salt pool of the Great Sea, wash their armour, for these?

I promised in my last letter that I would tell you the main meaning and bearing of the war, and its results to this day:—now that you know what Communism is, I can tell you these briefly, and, what is more to the purpose, how to bear yourself in the midst of them.

The first reason for all wars, and for the necessity of national defences, is that the majority of persons, high and low, in all European nations, are Thieves, and, in their hearts, greedy of their neighbours' goods, land, and fame.

But besides being Thieves, they are also fools, and have never yet been able to understand that if Cornish men want pippins cheap, they must not ravage Devonshire—that the prosperity of their neighbours is, in the end, their own also; and the poverty of their neighbours, by the communism of God, becomes also in the end their own. 'Invidia,' jealousy of your neighbour's good, has been, since dust was first made flesh, the curse of man; and 'Charitas,' the desire to do your neighbour grace, the one source of all human glory, power, and material Blessing.

But war between nations (fools and thieves though they be,) is not necessarily in all respects evil. I gave you that long extract from Froissart to show you, mainly, that Theft in its simplicity—however sharp and rude, yet if frankly done, and bravely—does not corrupt men's souls ; and they can, in a foolish, but quite vital and faithful way, keep the feast of the Virgin Mary in the midst of it.

But Occult Theft,—Theft which hides itself even from itself, and is legal, respectable, and cowardly,—corrupts the body and soul of man, to the last fibre of them. And the guilty Thieves of Europe, the real sources of all deadly war in it, are the Capitalists—that is to say, people who live by percentages or the labour of others ; instead of by fair wages for their own. The *Real* war in Europe, of which this fighting in Paris is the Inauguration, is between these and the workman, such as these have made him. They have kept him poor, ignorant, and sinful, that they might, without his knowledge, gather for themselves the produce of his toil. At last, a dim insight into the fact of this dawns on him ; and such as they have made him he meets them, and *will* meet.

Nay, the time is even come when he will study that Meteorological question, suggested by the Spectator, formerly quoted, of the Filtration of Money from above downwards.

"It was one of the many delusions of the Commune," (says to-day's Telegraph, 24th June,) "that it could do without rich consumers." Well, such unconsumed existence would be very wonderful ! Yet it is, to me also, conceivable. Without the riches,—no ; but without the consumers ?—possibly ! It is occurring to the minds of the workmen that these Golden Fleeces must get their dew from somewhere. " Shall there be dew upon the fleece only ? " they ask :—and will be answered. They cannot do without these long purses, say you ? No ; but they want to find where the long purses are filled. Nay, even their trying to burn the Louvre, without reference to Art Professors, had a ray of meaning in it —quite Spectatorial

" If we must choose between a Titian and a Lanca-shire cotton-mill," (wrote the Spectator of August oth, last year, instructing me in political economy; just as the war was beginning,) " in the name of manhood and morality, give us the cotton-mill."

So thinks the French workman also, energetically ; only *his* mill is not to be in Lancashire. Both French and English agree to have no more Titians,—it is well, —but which is to have the Cotton-Mill ?

Do you see in the Times of yesterday and the day before, 22nd and 23rd June, that the Minister of France dares not, even in this her utmost need, put on an income tax ; and do you see why he dares not ?

Observe, such a tax is the only honest and just one ; because it tells on the rich in true proportion to the poor, and because it meets necessity in the shortest and bravest way, and without interfering with any com-mercial operation.

All rich people object to income tax, of course ;—they like to pay as much as a poor man pays on their tea, sugar, and tobacco,—nothing on their incomes.

Whereas, in true justice, the only honest and wholly right tax is one not merely on income, but property ; increasing in percentage as the property is greater. And the main virtue of such a tax is that it makes publicly known what every man has, and how he gets it.

For every kind of Vagabonds, high and low, agree in their dislike to give an account of the way they get their living ; still less, of how much they have got sewn up in their breeches. It does not, however, matter much to a country that it should know how its poor Vagabonds live ; but it is of vital moment that it should know how its rich Vagabonds live ; and that much of knowledge, it seems to me, in the present state of our education, is quite attainable. But that, when you have attained it, you may act on it wisely, the first need is that you should be sure you are living honestly yourselves. That is why I told you, in my second letter, you must learn to obey good laws before you seek to alter bad ones :—I will amplify now a little the three promises I want you to make. Look back at them.

I. You are to do good work, whether you live or die. It may be you will have to die ;—well, men have died for their country often, yet doing her no good ; be ready to die for her in doing her assured good : her, and all other countries with her.　Mind your own business with your absolute heart and soul ; but see that it is a good business first.　That it *is* corn and sweet pease you are producing,—not gunpowder and arsenic.　And be sure of this, literally :—*you must simply rather die than make any destroying mechanism or compound.*　You are to be *literally* employed in cultivating the ground, or making useful things, and carrying them where they are wanted. Stand in the streets, and say to all who pass by : Have you any vineyard we can work in,—*not* Naboth's ?　In your powder and petroleum manufactory, we work no more.

I have said little to you yet of any of the pictures engraved—you perhaps think, not to the ornament of my book.

Be it so.　You will find them better than ornaments in time.　Notice, however, in the one I give you with this letter—the " Charity " of Giotto—the Red Queen of Dante, and ours also,—how different his thought of her is from the common one.

Usually she is nursing children, or giving money. Giotto thinks there is little charity in nursing children ; —bears and wolves do that for their little ones ; and less still in giving money.

His Charity tramples upon bags of gold—has no use for them.　She gives only corn and flowers ; and God's angel gives *her*, not even these—but a Heart.

Giotto is quite literal in his meaning, as well as figurative. Your love is to give food and flowers, and to labour for them only.

But what are we to do against powder and petroleum, then? What men may do; not what poisonous beasts may. If a wretch spit in your face, will you answer by spitting in his?—if he throw vitriol at you, will you go to the apothecary for a bigger bottle?

There is no physical crime at this day, so far beyond pardon,—so without parallel in its untempted guilt, as the making of war-machinery, and invention of mischievous substance. Two nations may go mad, and fight like harlots—God have mercy on them;—you, who hand them carving-knives off the table, for leave to pick up a dropped sixpence, what mercy is there for *you*? We are so humane, forsooth, and so wise; and our ancestors had tar-barrels for witches; *we* will have them for everybody else, and drive the witches' trade ourselves, by daylight; we will have our cauldrons, please Hecate, cooled (according to the Darwinian theory,) with baboon's blood, and enough of it, and sell hell-fire in the open street.

II. Seek to revenge no injury. You see now—do not you—a little more clearly why I wrote that? what strain there is on the untaught masses of you to revenge themselves, even with insane fire?

Alas, the Taught masses are strained enough also;— have you not just seen a great religious and reformed

nation, with its goodly Captains,—philosophical, senti-
mental, domestic, evangelical-angelical-minded altogether,
and with its Lord's Prayer really quite vital to it,—come
and take its neighbour nation by the throat, saying,
" Pay me that thou owest"?

Seek to revenge no injury : I do not say, seek to
punish no crime : look what I hinted about failed
bankers. Of that hereafter.

III. Learn to obey good laws ; and in a little while
you will reach the better learning—how to obey good
Men, who are living, breathing, unblinded law ; and to
subdue base and disloyal ones, recognizing in these the
light, and ruling over those in the power. of the Lord
of Light and Peace, whose Dominion is an everlasting
Dominion, and His Kingdom from generation to generation.

Ever faithfully yours,

JOHN RUSKIN.

FORS CLAVIGERA.

LETTER THE 8th.

NOT AS THE WORLD GIVES.

MY FRIENDS,

I begin this letter a month before it is wanted,* having several matters in my mind that I would fain put into words at once. It is the first of July, and I sit down to write by the dismallest light that ever yet I wrote by; namely, the light of this midsummer morning, in mid-England, (Matlock, Derbyshire,) in the year 1871.

For the sky is covered with grey cloud;—not rain-cloud, but a dry black veil, which no ray of sunshine can pierce; partly diffused in mist, feeble mist, enough to make distant objects unintelligible, yet without any substance, or wreathing, or colour of its own. And everywhere the leaves of the trees are shaking fitfully, as they

---

* I have since been ill, and cannot thoroughly revise my sheets; but my good friend Mr. Robert Chester, whose keen reading has saved me many a blunder ere now, will, I doubt not, see me safely through the pinch.

do before a thunderstorm ; only not violently, but enough
to show the passing to and fro of a strange, bitter,
blighting wind. Dismal enough, had it been the first
morning of its kind that summer had sent. But during
all this spring, in London, and at Oxford, through
meagre March, through changelessly sullen April, through
despondent May, and darkened June, morning after
morning has come grey-shrouded thus.

And it is a new thing to me, and a very dreadful one.
I am fifty years old, and more ; and since I was five, have
gleaned the best hours of my life in the sun of spring
and summer mornings ; and I never saw such as these,
till now.

And the scientific men are busy as ants, examining
the sun, and the moon, and the seven stars, and can tell
me all about *them*, I believe, by this time ; and how they
move, and what they are made of.

And I do not care, for my part, two copper spangles
how they move, nor what they are made of. I can't move
them any other way than they go, nor make them of
anything else, better than they are made. But I would
care much and give much, if I could be told where this
bitter wind comes from, and what *it* is made of.

For, perhaps, with forethought, and fine laboratory
science, one might make it of something else.

It looks partly as if it were made of poisonous smoke ;
very possibly it may be : there are at least two hundred
furnace chimneys in a square of two miles on every side

of me. But mere smoke would not blow to and fro in that wild way. It looks more to me as if it were made of dead men's souls—such of them as are not gone yet where they have to go, and may be flitting hither and thither, doubting, themselves, of the fittest place for them.

You know, if there *are* such things as souls, and if ever any of them haunt places where they have been hurt, there must be many about us, just now, displeased enough !

You may laugh, if you like. I don't believe any one of you would like to live in a room with a murdered man in the cupboard, however well preserved chemically ; —even with a sunflower growing out at the top of his head.

And I don't, myself, like living in a world with such a multitude of murdered men in the ground of it—though we *are* making heliotropes of them, and scientific flowers, that study the sun.

I wish the scientific men would let me and other people study it with our own eyes, and neither through telescopes nor heliotropes. You shall, at all events, study the rain a little, if not the sun, to-day, and settle that question we have been upon so long as to where it comes from.

All France, it seems, is in a state of enthusiastic delight and pride at the unexpected facility with which she has got into debt ; and Monsieur Thiers is congratulated by all our wisest papers on his beautiful statesmanship of borrowing. I don't myself see the cleverness of it, having suffered a good deal from that kind of statesmanship in private persons: but I daresay it is as clever as anything else that statesmen do, now-a-days ; only it happens to be more mischievous than most of their other doings, and I want you to understand the bearings of it.

Everybody in France who has got any money is eager to lend it to M. Thiers at five per cent. · No doubt ; but who is to pay the five per cent.? It is to be " raised " by duties on this and that. Then certainly the persons who get the five per cent. will have to pay some part of these duties themselves, on their own tea and sugar, or whatever else is taxed ; and this taxing will be on the whole of their trade, and on whatever they buy with the rest of their fortunes ; * but the five per cent. only on what they lend M. Thiers.

---

* "The charge on France for the interest of the newly-created debt, for the amount advanced by the Bank, and for the annual repayments—in short, for the whole additional burdens which the war has rendered necessary—is substantially to be met by increased Customs and Excise duties. The two principles which seem to have governed the selection of these imposts are, to extort the largest amount of money as it is leaving the hand of the purchaser, and to enforce the same process as the cash is falling into the hand of the native vendor ; the results being to burden the consumer and restrict the nat'onal industry. Leading commodities of necessary use—such as sugar and coffee, all raw materials for manufacture, and all textile substances—have to pay *ad valorem* duties, in some cases ruinously heavy. Worse still, and bearing most seriously on English interests, heavy export duties are to be imposed on French products, among which wine, brandy, liqueurs, fruits, eggs, and oilcake stand conspicuous—these articles paying a fixed duty ; while all others, grain and flour, we presume, included, will pay 1 per cent. *ad valorem*. Navigation dues are also to be levied on shipping, French and

It is a low estimate to say the payment of duties will take off one per cent. of their five.

Practically, therefore, the arrangement is that they get four per cent. for their money, and have all the trouble of customs duties, to take from them another extra one per cent., and give it them back again. Four per cent., however, is not to be despised. But who pays *that?*

The people who have got no money to lend, pay it; the daily worker and producer pays it. Unfortunate "William," who has borrowed, in this instance, not a

---

foreign; and the internal postage of letters is to be increased 25 per cent. From the changes in the Customs duties alone an increased revenue of £10,500,000 is anticipated. We will not venture to assert that these changes may not yield the amount of money so urgently needed ; but if they do, the result will open up a new chapter in political economy. Judging from the experience of every civilised State, it is simply inconceivable that such a tariff can be productive, can possess the faculty of healthy natural increase, or can act otherwise than as a dead weight on the industrial energies of the country. Every native of France will have to pay more for articles of prime necessity, and will thus have less to spare on articles of luxury —that is, on those which contribute most to the revenue, with the least of damage to the resources of his industry. Again, the manufacturer will have the raw material of his trade enhanced in value ; and, though he may have the benefit of a drawback on his exports, he will find his home market starved by State policy. His foreign customer will purchase less, because the cost is so much greater, and because his means are lessened by the increase in the prices of food through the export duty on French products. The French peasant finds *his* market contracted by an export duty which prevents the English consumers of his eggs, poultry, and wine from buying as largely as they once did ; his profits are therefore reduced, his piece of ground is less valuable, his ability to pay taxes is lessened. The policy, in short, might almost be thought expressly devised to impoverish the entire nation when it most wants enriching—to strangle French industry by slow degrees, to dry up at their source the main currents of revenue. Our only hope is, that the proposals, by their very grossness, will defeat themselves."— *Telegraph, June 29th.*

plane he could make planks with, but mitrailleuses and gunpowder, with which he has planed away his own farm-steads, and forests, and fair fields of corn, and having left himself desolate, now has to pay for the loan of this useful instrument, five per cent. So says the gently commercial James to him : "Not only the price of your plane, but five per cent. to me for lending it, O sweetest of Williams."

Sweet William, carrying generally more absinthe in his brains than wit, has little to say for himself, having, indeed, wasted too much of his sweetness lately, tainted disagreeably with petroleum, on the desert air of Paris. And the people who are to get their five per cent. out of him, and roll him and suck him,—the sugar-cane of a William that he is,—how should they but think the arrangement a glorious one for the nation ?

So there is great acclaim and triumphal procession of financiers ! and the arrangement is made ; namely, that all the poor labouring persons in France are to pay the rich idle ones five per cent. annually, on the sum of eighty millions of sterling pounds, until further notice.

But this is not all, observe. Sweet William is not altogether so soft in his rind that you can crush him without some sufficient machinery : you must have your army in good order, "to justify public confidence ;" and you must get the expense of that, beside your five per cent., out of ambrosial William. He must pay the cost of his own roller.

Now, therefore, see briefly what it all comes to.

First, you spend eighty millions of money in fireworks, doing no end of damage in letting them off.

Then you borrow money, to pay the firework-maker's bill, from any gain-loving persons who have got it.

And then, dressing your bailiff's men in new red coats and cocked hats, you send them drumming and trumpeting into the fields, to take the peasants by the throat, and make them pay the interest on what you have borrowed ; and the expense of the cocked hats besides.

That is " financiering," my friends, as the mob of the money-makers understand it. And they understand it well. For that is what it always comes to, finally ; taking the peasant by the throat. He *must* pay—for he only *can*. Food can only be got out of the ground, and all these devices of soldiership, and law, and arithmetic, are but ways of getting at last down to him, the furrow-driver, and snatching the roots from him as he digs.

And they have got him down, now, they think, well, for a while, poor William, after his fit of fury and petroleum : and can make their money out of him for years to come, in the old ways.

Did you chance, my friends, any of you, to see, the other day, the 83rd number of the Graphic, with the picture of the Queen's concert in it ? All the fine ladies sitting so trimly, and looking so sweet, and doing the whole

duty of woman—wearing their fine clothes gracefully;
and the pretty singer, white-throated, warbling "Home,
sweet home" to them, so morally, and melodiously!
Here was yet to be our ideal of virtuous life, thought
the Graphic! Surely, we are safe back with our virtues
in satin slippers and lace veils;—and our Kingdom of
Heaven is come again, *with* observation, and crown diamonds of the dazzlingest. Cherubim and Seraphim in
toilettes de Paris,—(blue-de-ciel—vert d'olivier-de—Noé—
mauve de colombe-fusillée,) dancing to Coote and Tinney's
band; and vulgar Hell reserved for the canaille, as
heretofore! Vulgar Hell shall be didactically pour-
trayed, accordingly; (see page 17,)—Wickedness going
its way to *its* poor Home—bitter-sweet. Ouvrier and
pétroleuse—prisoners at last—glaring wild on their way
to die.

Alas! of these divided races, of whom one was appointed to teach and guide the other, which has indeed
sinned deepest—the unteaching, or the untaught?—which
now are guiltiest—these, who perish, or those—who forget?

Ouvrier and pétroleuse; they are gone their way—
to their death. But for these, the Virgin of France shall
yet unfold the oriflamme above their graves, and lay her
blanched lilies on their smirched dust. Yes, and for these,
great Charles shall rouse his Roland, and bid him put
ghostly trump to lip, and breathe a point of war; and
the helmed Pucelle shall answer with a wood-note of
Domrémy;—yes, and for these the Louis they mocked,

like his master, shall raise his holy hands, and pray God's peace.

"Not as the world giveth." Everlasting shame only, and unrest, are the world's gifts. These Swine of the five per cent. shall share them duly.

> La sconoscente vita, che i fe' sozzi
> Ad ogni conoscenza or li fa bruni.
> *   *   *   *
> Che tutto l'oro, ch'e sotto la luna,
> E che già fù, di queste anime stanche
> Non poterebbe farne posar una.

"Ad ogni conoscenza bruni:" Dark to all recognition! So they would have it indeed, true of instinct. "Ce serait l'inquisition," screamed the Senate of France, threatened with income-tax and inquiry into their ways and means. Well,—what better thing could it be? Had they not been blind long enough, under their mole-hillocks, that they should shriek at the first spark of "Inquisition"? A few things might be "inquired," one should think, and answered, among honest men, now, to advantage, and openly? "Ah no—for God's sake," shrieks the Senate, "no Inquisition. If ever anybody should come to know how we live, we were disgraced for ever, honest gentlemen that we are."

Now, my friends, the first condition of all bravery is to keep out of *this* loathsomeness. If you *do* live by rapine, stand up like a man for the old law of bow and spear; but don't fall whimpering down on your belly, like Autolycus, "grovelling on the ground," when

another human creature asks you how you get your
daily bread, with an " Oh, that ever I was born,—here
is inquisition come on me!"

The Inquisition must come. Into men's consciences,
no; not now: there is little worth looking into there.
But into their pockets—yes; a most practicable and
beneficial inquisition, to be made thoroughly and pur-
gatorially, once for all, and rendered unnecessary hereafter. by furnishing the relieved marsupialia with—*glass*
pockets, for the future.

You know, at least, that we, in our own society, are
to have glass pockets, as we are all to give the tenth of
what we have, to buy land with, so that we must every
one know each other's property to a farthing. And this
month I begin making up my own accounts for you,
as I said I would : I could not, sooner, though I set
matters in train as soon as my first letter was out, and
effected (as I supposed !), in February, a sale of 14,000*l.*
worth of houses, at the West End, to Messrs. —— and
——, of —— Row.

But from then till now, I've been trying to get that
piece of business settled, and until yesterday, 19th July,
I have not been able.

For, first there was a mistake made by my lawyer in
the list of the houses : No. 7 ought to have been No. 1.
It was a sheer piece of stupidity, and ought to have
been corrected by a dash of the pen ; but all sorts of
deeds had to be made out again, merely that they might

be paid for ; and it took about three months to change 7 into 1.

At last all was declared smooth again, and I thought I should get my money ; but Messrs. —— never stirred. My people kept sending them letters, saying I really did want the money, though they mightn't think it. Whether they thought it or not, they took no notice of any such informal communications. I thought they were going to back out of their bargain ; but my man of business at last got their guarantee for its completion.

"If they've guaranteed the payment, why don't they pay ?" thought I ; but still I couldn't get any money. At last I found the lawyers on both sides were quarrelling over the stamp-duties ! Nobody knew, of the whole pack of them, whether this stamp or that was the right one ! and my lawyers wouldn't give an eighty-pound stamp, and theirs wouldn't be content with a twenty-pound one.

Now, you know, all this stamp business itself is merely Mr. Gladstone's * way of coming in for *his* share of the booty. I can't be allowed to sell my houses in peace, but Mr. Gladstone must have his three hundred pounds out of me, to feed his Woolwich infant with, and fire it off " with the most satisfactory result," " nothing damaged but the platform."

I am content, if only he would come and say what

---

* Of course the Prime Minister is always the *real* tax-gatherer ; the Chancellor of the Exchequer is only the cat's-paw.

he wants, and take it, and get out of my sight. But not to know what he *does* want! and to keep me from getting my money at all, while his lawyers are asking which is the right stamp? I think he had better be clear on that point next time.

But here, at last, are six months come and gone, and the stamp question is—not settled, indeed, but I've undertaken to keep my man of business free of harm, if the stamps won't do; and so at last he says I'm to have my money; and I really believe, by the time this letter is out, Messrs. —— will have paid me my 14,000*l.*

Now you know I promised you the tenth of all I had, when free from incumbrances already existing on it. This first instalment of 14,000*l.* is not all clear, for I want part of it to found a Mastership of Drawing under the Art Professorship at Oxford; which I can't do rightly for less than 5,000*l.* But I'll count the sum left as 10,000*l.* instead of 9,000*l.*, and that will be clear for our society, and so, you shall have a thousand pounds down, as the tenth of that, which will quit me, observe, of my pledge thus far.

A thousand *down*, I say; but down where? Where can I put it to be safe for us? You will find presently, as others come in to help us, and we get something worth taking care of, that it becomes a very curious question indeed, where we can put our money to be safe!

In the meantime, I've told my man of business to buy 1,000*l.* consols in the names of two men of honour; the names cannot yet be certain. What remains of the round thousand shall be kept to add to next instalment. And thus begins the fund, which I think we may advisably call the " St. George's " fund. And although the interest on consols is, as I told you before, only the taxation on the British peasant continued since the Napoleon wars, still *this* little portion of his labour, the interest on our St. George's fund, will at last be saved for him, and brought back to him.

And now, if you will read over once again the end of my fifth letter, I will tell you a little more of what we are to do with this money, as it increases.

First, let whoever gives us any, be clear in their minds that it is a Gift. It is not an Investment. It is a frank and simple gift to the British people : nothing of it is to come back to the giver.

But also, nothing of it is to be lost. The money is not to be spent in feeding Woolwich infants with gunpowder. It is to be spent in dressing the earth and keeping it,— in feeding human lips,—in clothing human bodies,—in kindling human souls.

First of all, I say, in dressing the earth. As soon as the fund reaches any sufficient amount, the Trustees shall buy with it any kind of land offered them at just price in Britain. Rock, moor, marsh, or sea-shore—it matters not what, so it be British ground, and secured to us.

Then, we will ascertain the absolute best that can be made of every acre. We will first examine what flowers and herbs it naturally bears; every wholesome flower that it will grow shall be sown in its wild places, and every kind of fruit-tree that can prosper; and arable and pasture land extended by every expedient of tillage, with humble and simple cottage dwellings under faultless sanitary regulation. Whatever piece of land we begin to work upon, we shall treat thoroughly at once, putting unlimited manual labour on it, until we have every foot of it under as strict care as a flower-garden: and the labourers shall be paid sufficient, unchanging wages; and their children educated compulsorily in agricultural schools inland, and naval schools by the sea, the indispensable first condition of such education being that the boys learn either to ride or to sail; the girls to spin, weave, and sew, and at a proper age to cook all ordinary food exquisitely; the youth of both sexes to be disciplined daily in the strictest practice of vocal music; and for morality, to be taught gentleness to all brute creatures,—finished courtesy to each other,—to speak truth with rigid care, and to obey orders with the precision of slaves. Then, as they get older, they are to learn the natural history of the place they live in,—to know Latin, boys and girls both, —and the history of five cities: Athens, Rome, Venice, Florence, and London.

Now, as I told you in my fifth letter, to what extent I may be able to carry this plan into execution, I know not; but to *some* visible extent, with my own single hand, I can and will, if I live. Nor do I doubt but that I shall find help enough, as soon as the full action of the system is seen, and ever so little a space of rightly cultivated ground in perfect beauty, with inhabitants in peace of heart, of whom none

> Doluit miserans inopem, aut invidit habenti.

Such a life we have lately been taught by vile persons to think impossible; so far from being impossible, it *has* been the actual life of all glorious human states in their origin.

> Hanc olim veteres vitam coluere Sabini ;
> Hanc Remus et frater ; sic fortis Etruria crevit ;
> Scilicet et rerum facta est pulcherrima Roma.

But, had it never been endeavoured until now, we might yet learn to hope for its unimagined good by considering what it has been possible for us to reach of unimagined evil. Utopia and its benediction are probable and simple things, compared to the Kakotopia and its curse, which we had seen actually fulfilled. We have seen the city of Paris (what miracle can be thought of beyond this?) with her own forts raining ruin on her palaces, and her young children casting fire into the streets in which they had been born, but we have not faith enough in heaven to imagine the reverse of this, or the building of any city whose streets shall be full of innocent boys and girls playing in the midst thereof.

My friends, you have trusted, in your time, too many idle words. Read now these following, not idle ones ;

and remember *them ;* and trust them, for they are true :—

" Oh, thou afflicted, tossed with tempest, **and** not comforted, behold, I will lay thy stones with fair colours, and lay thy foundations with sapphires.

" And all thy children shall be taught of the Lord ; and great shall be the peace of thy children.

" In righteousness shalt thou be established : thou shalt be far from oppression ; for thou shalt not fear and from terror ; for it shall not come near thee. . . .

" Whosoever shall gather together against thee shall fall for thy sake. . . .

" No weapon that is formed against thee shall prosper ; and every tongue that shall rise against thee in judgment thou shalt condemn.   This is the heritage of the servants of the Lord ; and their righteousness is of me, saith the Lord."

Remember only that in this now antiquated translation, " righteousness" means, accurately and simply, " justice," and is the eternal law of right, obeyed alike in the great times of each state, by Jew, Greek, and Roman.   In my next letter, we will examine into the nature of this justice, and of its relation to Governments that deserve the name.

And so believe me

Faithfully yours,

JOHN RUSKIN.

FORS CLAVIGERA.

LETTER THE 9th.

HONOUR TO WHOM HONOUR.

DENMARK HILL,
1st September, 1871.

MY FRIENDS,

As the design which I had in view when I began these letters (and many a year before, in the germ and first outlines of it) is now fairly afoot, and in slow, but determined, beginning of realization, I will endeavour in this and the next following letter to set its main features completely before you ; though, remember, the design would certainly be a shallow and vain one, if its bearings could be either shortly explained, or quickly understood. I have much in my own hope, which I know you are as yet incapable of hoping, but which your enemies are dexterous in discouraging, and eager to discourage. Have you noticed how curiously and earnestly the greater number of public journals that have yet quoted these papers, allege, for their part, nothing but the difficulties in our way ; and that with as much contempt as they can venture to express ? No editor could say to your face that the endeavour to give you fresh air, wholesome employment, and high education, was reprehensible or dangerous. The worst he can venture to say is, that it is ridiculous,—which you observe is, by most, declared as wittily as they may.

Some must, indeed, candidly think, as well as say so. Education of any noble kind has of late been so constantly given only to the idle classes, or, at least, to those who conceive it a privilege to be idle,* that it is difficult for any person, trained in modern habits of thought, to imagine a true and refined scholarship, of which the essential foundation is to be skill in some useful labour. Time and trial will show which of the two conceptions of education is indeed the ridiculous one—and *have* shown, many and many a day before this, if any one would look at the showing. Such trial, however, I mean anew to make, with what life is left to me, and help given to me : and the manner of it is to be this, that, few or many, as our company may be, we will secure for the people of Britain as wide spaces of British ground as we can ; and on such spaces of freehold land

---

* Infinite nonsense is talked about the "work done" by the upper classes. I have done a little myself, in my day, of the kind of work they boast of ; but mine, at least, has been all play. Even lawyer's, which is, on the whole, the hardest, you may observe to be essentially grim play, made more jovial for themselves by conditions which make it somewhat dismal to other people. Here and there we have a real worker among soldiers, or no soldiering would long be possible ; nevertheless young men don't go into the Guards with any primal or essential idea of work.

we will cause to be trained as many British children as we can, in healthy, brave, and kindly life, to every one of whom there shall be done true justice, and dealt fair opportunity of " advancement," or what else may, indeed, be good for them.

" True justice!" I might more shortly have written " justice," only you are all now so much in the way of asking for what you think " rights," which, if you could get them, would turn out to be the deadliest wrongs; —and you suffer so much from an external mechanism of justice, which for centuries back has abetted, or, at best, resulted in, every conceivable manner of injustice —that I am compelled to say " *True* justice," to distinguish it from that which is commonly imagined by the populace, or attainable under the existing laws, of civilized nations.

This true justice—(not to spend time, which I am apt to be too fond of doing, in verbal definition), consists mainly in the granting to every human being due aid in the development of such faculties as it possesses for action and enjoyment; primarily, for useful action, because all enjoyment worth having (nay, all enjoyment not harmful) must in some way arise out of that, either in happy energy, or rightly complacent and exulting rest.

" Due " aid, you see, I have written. Not " equal " aid. One of the first statements I made to you respecting this domain of ours was " there shall be no equality in it." In education especially, true justice is curiously unequal—if you choose to give it a hard name, iniquitous. The right law of it is that you are to take most pains with the best material. Many conscientious masters will plead for the exactly contrary iniquity, and say you should take the most pains with the dullest boys. But that is not so (only you must be very careful that you know which *are* the dull boys ; for the cleverest look often very like them). Never waste pains on bad ground ; let it remain rough, though properly looked after and cared for ; it will be of best service so ; but spare no labour on the good, or on what has in it the capacity of good. The tendency of modern help and care is quite morbidly and madly in reverse of this great principle. Benevolent persons are always, by preference, busy on the essentially bad ; and exhaust themselves in efforts to get maximum intellect from cretins, and maximum virtue from criminals. Meantime, they take no care to ascertain (and for the most part when ascertained, obstinately refuse to remove) the continuous sources of cretinism and crime, and suffer the most splendid material in child-nature to wander neglected about the streets, until it has become rotten to the degree in which they feel prompted to take an interest in it. Now I have not the slightest intention —understand this, I beg of you, very clearly—of setting myself to mend or reform people ; when they are once out of form they may stay so, for me.* But of what

---

* I speak in the first person, not insolently, but necessarily, being yet alone in this design : and for some time to come the responsibility of carrying it on

unspoiled stuff I can find to my hand I will cut the best shapes there is room for : shapes unalterable, if it may be, for ever.

" The best shapes there is room for," since, according to the conditions around them, men's natures must expand or remain contracted ; and, yet more distinctly, let me say, " the best shapes that there is *substance* for," seeing that we must accept contentedly infinite difference in the original nature and capacity, even at their purest ; which it is the first condition of right education to make manifest to all persons—most of all to the persons chiefly concerned. That other men should know their measure, is, indeed, desirable ; but that they should know it themselves, is wholly necessary.

" By competitive examination of course ? " Sternly, no ! but under absolute prohibition of all violent and strained effort—most of all envious or anxious effort— in every exercise of body and mind ; and by enforcing on every scholar's heart, from the first to the last stage of his instruction, the irrevocable ordinance of the third Fors Clavigera, that his mental rank among men is fixed from the hour he was born,—that by no temporary or

must rest with me, nor do I ask or desire any present help, except from those who understand what I have written in the course of the last ten years, and who can trust me, therefore. But the continuance of the scheme must depend on the finding men staunch and prudent for the heads of each department of the practical work, consenting, indeed, with each other as to certain great principles of that work, but left wholly to their own judgment as to the manner and degree in which they are to be carried into effect.

violent effort can he train, though he may seriously injure
the faculties he has ; that by no manner of effort can he
increase them ; and that his best happiness is to consist
in the admiration of powers by him for ever unattainable,
and of arts, and deeds, by him ever inimitable.

Some ten or twelve years ago, when I was first actively
engaged in Art teaching, a young Scottish student came
up to London to put himself under me, having taken
many prizes (justly, with respect to the qualities looked
for by the judges) in various schools of Art. He worked
under me very earnestly and patiently for some time ;
and I was able to praise his doings in what I thought
very high terms : nevertheless, there remained always a
look of mortification on his face, after he had been
praised, however unqualifiedly. At last, he could hold
no longer, but one day, when I had been more than
usually complimentary, turned to me with an anxious,
yet not unconfident expression, and asked : " Do you
think, sir, that I shall ever draw as well as Turner ? "

I paused for a second or two, being much taken aback ;
and then answered,* " It is far more likely you should
be made Emperor of All the Russias. There is a new
Emperor every fifteen or twenty years, on the average ;
and by strange hap, and fortunate cabal, anybody might
be made Emperor. But there is only one Turner in five

---

* I do not mean that I answered in these words, but to the effect of them,
at greater length.

hundred years, and God decides, without any admission of auxiliary cabal, what piece of clay His soul is to be put in."

It was the first time that I had been brought into direct collision with the modern system of prize-giving and competition ; and the mischief of it was, in the sequel, clearly shown to me, and tragically. This youth had the finest powers of mechanical execution I have ever met with, but was quite incapable of invention, or strong intellectual effort of any kind. Had he been taught early and thoroughly to know his place, and be content with his faculty, he would have been one of the happiest and most serviceable of men. But, at the Art schools, he got prize after prize for his neat handling ; and having, in his restricted imagination, no power of discerning the qualities of great work, all the vanity of his nature was brought out unchecked ; so that, being intensely industrious and conscientious, as well as vain (it is a Scottish combination of character not unfrequent,*) he naturally expected to become one of the greatest of men. My answer not only mortified, but angered him, and made him suspicious of me ; he thought I wanted to keep his talents from being fairly displayed, and soon afterwards asked leave (he was then in my employment

---

* We English are usually bad altogether in a 'harmonious way, and only quite insolent when we are quite good-for-nothing; the least good in us shows itself in a measure of modesty; but many Scotch natures, of fine capacity otherwise, are rendered entirely abortive by conceit.

as well as under my teaching) to put himself under another master. I gave him leave at once, telling him, " if he found the other master no better to his mind, he might come back to me whenever he chose." The other master giving him no more hope of advancement than I did, he came back to me ; I sent him into Switzerland, to draw Swiss architecture ; but instead of doing what I bid him, quietly, and nothing else, he set himself, with furious industry, to draw snowy mountains and clouds, that he might show me he *could* draw like Albert Dürer, or Turner ;—spent his strength in agony of vain effort ;—caught cold, fell into decline, and died. How many actual deaths are now annually caused by the strain and anxiety of competitive examination, it would startle us all if we could know : but the mischief done to the best faculties of the brain in all cases, and the miserable confusion and absurdity involved in the system itself, which offers every place, not to the man who is indeed fitted for it, but to the one who, on a given day, chances to have bodily strength enough to stand the cruellest strain, are evils infinite in their con-sequences, and more lamentable than many deaths.

This, then, shall be the first condition of what educa-tion it may become possible for us to give, that the strength of the youths shall never be strained ; and that their best powers shall be developed in each, without competition, though they shall have to pass crucial, but not severe, examinations, attesting clearly to themselves and to other people, not the utmost they can do, but that at least they can do *some* things accurately and well : their own certainty of this being accompanied with the quite as clear and much happier certainty, that there are many other things which they will never be able to do at all.

"The happier certainty ?" Yes. A man's happiness consists infinitely more in admiration of the faculties of others than in confidence in his own. That reverent admiration is the perfect human gift in him ; all lower animals are happy and noble in the degree they can share it. A dog reverences you, a fly does not ; the capacity of partly understanding a creature above him, is the dog's nobility. Increase such reverence in human beings, and you increase daily their happiness, peace, and dignity ; take it away, and you make them wretched as well as vile. But for fifty years back modern education has devoted itself simply to the teaching of impudence ; and then we complain that we can no more manage our mobs ! "Look at Mr. Robert Stephenson," (we tell a boy,) "and at Mr. James Watt, and Mr. William Shakspeare ! You know you are every bit as good as they ; you have only to work in the same way, and you will infallibly arrive at the same eminence." Most boys believe the "you are every bit as good as they," without any painful experiment : but the better-minded ones really take the advised measures ; and as, at the end of all things, there *can* be but one Mr. James Watt or

Mr. William Shakspeare, the rest of the candidates for distinction, finding themselves, after all their work, still indistinct, think it must be the fault of the police, and are riotous accordingly.

To some extent it *is* the fault of the police, truly enough, considering as the police of Europe, or teachers of politeness and civic manners, its higher classes,— higher either by race or faculty. Police they are, or else are nothing: bound to keep order, both by clear teaching of the duty and delight of Respect, and, much more, by being themselves—Respectable; whether as priests, or kings, or lords, or generals, or admirals; —if they will only take care to be verily *that*, the Respect will be forthcoming, with little pains: nay, even Obedience, inconceivable to modern free souls as it may be, we shall get again, as soon as there is anybody worth obeying, and who can keep us out of shoal water.

Not but that those two admirals and their captains have been sorely, though needfully, dealt with. It was, doubtless, not a scene of the brightest in our naval history—that *Agincourt*, entomologically, as it were, pinned to her wrong place, off Gibraltar; but in truth, it was less the captain's fault, than the ironmonger's. You need not think you can ever have seamen in iron ships; it is not in flesh and blood to be vigilant when vigilance is so slightly necessary: the best seaman born will lose his qualities, when he knows he can steam against wind and tide,* and has to handle ships so large that the care of them is necessarily divided among many persons. If you want sea-captains indeed, like Sir Richard Grenville or Lord Dundonald, you must give them small ships, and wooden ones,—nothing but oak, pine, and hemp to trust to, above or below,—and those, trustworthy.

You little know how much is implied in the two conditions of boys' education that I gave you in my last letter, —that they shall all learn either to ride or sail; nor by what constancy of law the power of highest discipline and honour is vested by Nature in the two chivalries— of the Horse and the Wave. Both are significative of the right command of man over his own passions; but they teach, farther, the strange mystery of relation that exists between his soul and the wild natural elements on the one hand, and the wild lower animals on the other. The sea-riding gave their chief strength of temper to the Athenian, Norman, Pisan, and Venetian,—masters of the arts of the world : but the gentleness of chivalry, properly so called, depends on the recognition of the order and awe of lower and loftier animal-life, first clearly taught in the myth of Chiron, and in his bringing up of Jason, Æsculapius, and Achilles, but most perfectly by Homer in the fable of the horses of Achilles, and the part

---

* "Steam has, of course, utterly extirpated seamanship," says Admiral Rous, in his letter to 'The Times' (which I had, of course, not seen when I wrote this). Read the whole letter and the article on it in 'The Times' of the 17th, which is entirely temperate and conclusive.

assigned to them, in relation to the death of his friend, and in prophecy of his own.   There is, perhaps, in all the 'Iliad' nothing more deep in significance—there is nothing in all literature more perfect in human tenderness, and honour for the mystery of inferior life,* than the verses that describe the sorrow of the divine horses at the death of Patroclus, and the comfort given them by the greatest of the gods.   You shall read Pope's translation ; it does not give you the manner of the original, but it entirely gives you the passion :—

> Meantime, at distance from the scene of blood,
> The pensive steeds of great Achilles stood ;
> Their godlike master slain before their eyes
> They wept, and shared in human miseries.
> In vain Automedon now shakes the rein,
> Now plies the lash, and soothes and threats in vain ;
> Nor to the fight nor Hellespont they go,
> Restive they stood, and obstinate in woe ;
> Still as a tombstone, never to be moved,
> On some good man or woman unreproved
> Lays its eternal weight ; or fix'd as stands
> A marble courser by the sculptor's hands,
> Placed on the hero's grave.   Along their face,
> The big round drops coursed down with silent pace,
> Conglobing on the dust.   Their manes, that late
> Circled their arched necks, and waved in state,
> Trail'd on the dust, beneath the yoke were spread,
> And prone to earth was hung their languid head :
> Nor Jove disdain'd to cast a pitying look,
> While thus relenting to the steeds he spoke :

---

* The myth of Balaam ; the cause assigned for the journey of the first King of Israel from his father's house ; and the manner of the triumphal entry of the greatest King of Judah into His capital, are symbolic of the same truths ; but in a yet more strange humility.

" Unhappy coursers of immortal strain !
Exempt from age, and deathless now in vain !
Did we your race on mortal man bestow,
Only, alas ! to share in mortal woe ?
For ah ! what is there, of inferior birth,
That breathes or creeps upon the dust of earth ;
What wretched creature of what wretched kind,
Than man more weak, calamitous and blind ?
A miserable race ! But cease to mourn !
For not by you shall Priam's son be borne
High on the splendid car ; one glorious prize
He rashly boasts ; the rest our will denies.
Ourself will swiftness to your nerves impart,
Ourself with rising spirits swell your heart.
Automedon your rapid flight shall bear
Safe to the navy through the storm of war. . . ."
   He said ; and, breathing in th' immortal horse
Excessive spirit, urged them to the course ;
From their high manes they shake the dust, and bear
The kindling chariot through the parted war.

Is not that a prettier notion of horses than you will
get from your betting English chivalry on the Derby
day ? * We will have, please heaven, some riding, not
as jockeys ride, and some sailing, not as pots and kettles
sail, once more on English land and sea ; and out of
both, kindled yet again, the chivalry of heart of the
Knight of Athens, and Eques of Rome, and Ritter of
Germany, and Chevalier of France, and Cavalier of
England—chivalry gentle always and lowly, among those
who deserved their name of knight ; showing mercy to
whom mercy was due, and honour to whom honour.

---

* Compare also Black Auster at the Battle of the Lake, in Macaulay's
' Lays of Rome.'

It exists yet, and out of La Mancha, too (or none of *us* could exist), whatever you may think in these days of ungentleness and Dishonour. It exists secretly, to the full, among you yourselves, and the recovery of it again would be to you as the opening of a well in the desert. You remember what I told you were the three spiritual treasures of your life—Admiration, Hope, and Love. Admiration is the Faculty of giving Honour. It is the best word we have for the various feelings of wonder, reverence, awe, and humility, which are needful for all lovely work, and which constitute the habitual temper of all noble and clear-sighted persons, as opposed to the " impudence " of base and blind ones. The Latins called this great virtue " pudor," of which our " impudence " is the negative ; the Greeks had a better word, " αἰδώς ; " too wide in the bearings of it for me to explain to you to-day, even if it *could* be explained before you recovered the feeling ;—which, after being taught for fifty years that impudence is the chief duty of man, and that living in coal-holes and ash-heaps is his proudest existence, and that the methods of generation of vermin are his loftiest subject of science,—it will not be easy for *you* to do ; but your children may, and you will see that it is good for them. In the history of the five cities I named, they shall learn, so far as they can understand, what has been beautifully and bravely done ; and they shall know the lives of the heroes and heroines in truth and naturalness ; and shall be taught to remember the greatest of them on the days of their birth and death ; so that the year shall have its full calendar of reverent Memory. And on every day, part of their morning service shall be a song in honour of the hero whose birthday it is : and part of their evening service, a song of triumph for the fair death of one whose death-day it is : and in their first learning of notes they shall be taught the great purpose of music, which is to say a thing that you mean deeply, in the strongest and clearest possible way ; and they shall never be taught to sing what they don't mean. They shall be able to sing merrily when they are happy, and earnestly when they are sad ; but they shall find no mirth in mockery, nor in obscenity ; neither shall they waste and profane their hearts with artificial and lascivious sorrow.

Regulations which will bring about some curious changes in piano-playing, and several other things.

"Which *will* bring." They are bold words, considering how many schemes have failed disastrously, (as your able editors gladly point out,) which seemed much more plausible than this. But, as far as I know history, good designs have not failed except when they were too narrow in their final aim, and too obstinately and eagerly pushed in the beginning of them. Prosperous Fortune only grants an almost invisible slowness of success, and demands invincible patience in pursuing it. Many good men have failed in haste ; more in egotism, and desire to keep everything in their own hands ; and some by

mistaking the signs of their times ; but others, and those
generally the boldest in imagination, have not failed ; and
their successors, true knights or monks, have bettered
the fate and raised the thoughts of men for centuries ;
nay, for decades of centuries. And there is assuredly
nothing in this purpose I lay before you, so far as it
reaches hitherto, which will require either knightly courage
or monkish enthusiasm to carry out. To divert a little
of the large current of English charity and justice from
watching disease to guarding health, and from the punish-
ment of crime to the reward of virtue ; to establish, here
and there, exercise grounds instead of hospitals, and
training schools instead of penitentiaries, is not, if you
will slowly take it to heart, a frantic imagination. What
farther hope I have of getting some honest men to serve,
each in his safe and useful trade, faithfully, as a good
soldier serves in his dangerous, and too often very wide
of useful one, may seem, for the moment, vain enough ;
for indeed, in the last sermon I heard out of an English
pulpit, the clergyman said it was now acknowledged to
be impossible for any honest man to live by trade in
England. From which the conclusion he drew was, not
that the manner of trade in England should be amended,
but that his hearers should be thankful they were going
to heaven. It never seemed to occur to him that perhaps
it might be only through amendment of their ways in trade
that some of them could ever get there.

Such madness, therefore, as may be implied in this

ultimate hope of seeing some honest work and traffic done in faithful fellowship, I confess to you : but what, for my own part, I am about to endeavour, is certainly within my power, if my life and health last a few years more, and the compass of it is soon definable. First, —as I told you at the beginning of these Letters,—I must do my own proper work as well as I can—nothing else must come in the way of that ; and for some time to come, it will be heavy, because, after carefully consider-ing the operation of the Kensington system of Art-teaching throughout the country, and watching for two years its effect on various classes of students at Oxford, I became finally convinced that it fell short of its objects in more than one vital particular : and I have, therefore, obtained permission to found a separate Mastership of Drawing in connection with the Art Professorship at Oxford ; and elementary schools will be opened in the University galleries, next October, in which the methods of teaching will be calculated to meet requirements which have not been contemplated in the Kensington system. But how far what these, not new, but very ancient, disciplines teach, may be by modern students, either required or endured, remains to be seen. The organization of the system of teaching, and preparation of examples, in this school, is, however, at present my chief work,—no light one,—and everything else must be subordinate to it.

But in my first series of lectures at Oxford, I stated (and cannot too often or too firmly state) that no great

arts were practicable by any people, unless they were
living contented lives, in pure air, out of the way of
unsightly objects, and emancipated from unnecessary
mechanical occupation. It is simply one part of the
practical work I have to do in Art-teaching, to bring,
somewhere, such conditions into existence, and to show
the working of them. I know also assuredly that the
conditions necessary for the Arts of men, are the best
for their souls and bodies; and knowing this, I do
not doubt but that it may be with due pains, to some
material extent, convincingly shown; and I am now
ready to receive help, little or much, from any one who
cares to forward the showing of it.

Sir Thomas Dyke Acland, and the Right Hon. William
Cowper-Temple, have consented to be the Trustees of the
fund; it being distinctly understood that in that office
they accept no responsibility for the conduct of the
scheme, and refrain from expressing any opinion of its
principles. They simply undertake the charge of the
money and land given to the St. George's Fund; certify
to the public that it is spent, or treated, for the purposes
of that fund, in the manner stated in my accounts of it;
and, in the event of my death, hold it for such fulfilment
of its purposes as they may then find possible.

But it is evidently necessary for the right working of
the scheme that the Trustees should not, except only in
that office, be at present concerned with or involved in
it; and that no ambiguous responsibility should fall on

them.   I know too much of the manner of law to hope
that I can get the arrangement put into proper form
before the end of the year ; but, I hope, at latest, on the
eve of Christmas Day (the day I named first) to publish
the December number of Fors with the legal terms all
clear : until then, whatever sums or land I may receive
will be simply paid to the Trustees, or secured in their
name, for the St. George's Fund ; what I may attempt
afterwards will be, in any case, scarcely noticeable for
some time ; for I shall only work with the interest of
the fund ; * and as I have strength and leisure :—I have
little enough of the one ; and am like to have little of
the other, for years to come, if these drawing-schools
become useful, as I hope.   But what I may do myself
is of small consequence.   Long before it can come to
any convincing result, I believe some of the gentlemen
of England will have taken up the matter, and seen
that, for their own sake, no less than the country's, they
must now live on their estates, not in shooting-time
only, but all the year ; and be themselves farmers, or
"shepherd lords," and make the field gain on the street,
not the street on the field ; and bid the light break into
the smoke-clouds, and bear in their hands, up to those

---

* Since last Fors was published I have sold some more property, which
has brought me in another ten thousand to tithe ; so that I have bought a
second thousand Consols in the names of the Trustees—and have received a
pretty little gift of seven acres of woodland. in Worcestershire, for you, already
—so you see there is at least a beginning.

loathsome city walls, the gifts of Giotto's Charity, corn and flowers.

It is time, too, I think. Did you notice the lovely instances of chivalry, modesty, and musical taste recorded in those letters in 'The Times,' giving description of the "civilizing" influence of our progressive age on the rural district of Margate?

They are of some documentary value, and worth preserving, for several reasons. Here they are :—

I.—A TRIP TO MARGATE.

To the Editor of "The Times."

Sir,—On Monday last I had the misfortune of taking a trip per steamer to Margate. The sea was rough, the ship crowded, and therefore most of the Cockney excursionists prostrate with sea-sickness. On landing on Margate pier I must confess I thought that, instead of landing in an English seaport, I had been transported by magic to a land inhabited by savages and lunatics. The scene that ensued when the unhappy passengers had to pass between the double line of a Margate mob on the pier must be seen to be believed possible in a civilized country. Shouts, yells, howls of delight greeted every pale-looking passenger, as he or she got on the pier, accompanied by a running comment of the lowest, foulest language imaginable. But the most insulted victims were a young lady, who having had a fit of hysterics on board, had to be assisted up the steps, and a venerable-looking old gentleman with a long grey beard, who, by-the-by, was not sick at all, but being crippled and very old, feebly tottered up the slippery steps leaning on two sticks. "Here's a guy!" "Hallo! you old thief, you won't get drowned, because you know that you are to be hung," etc., and worse than that, were the greetings of that poor old man. All this while a very much silver-bestriped policeman stood calmly by, without interfering by word or deed ; and myself, having several ladies to take care of, could do nothing except telling the ruffianly mob some hard words, with, of course, no other effect than to draw all the abuse on myself. This is not an exceptional exhibition of Margate ruffianism, but, as I have been told, is of daily occurrence, only varying in intensity with the roughness of the sea.

Public exposure is the only likely thing to put a stop to such ruffianism ; and now it is no longer a wonder to me why so many people are ashamed of confessing that they have been to Margate.

I remain, Sir, yours obediently,

·London, August 16.   C. L. S.

II.—MARGATE.

To the Editor of "The Times."

SIR,—From personal experience obtained from an enforced residence at Margate, I can confirm all that your correspondent "C. L. S." states of the behaviour of the mob on the jetty ; and in addition I will venture to say that in no town in England, or, so far as my experience goes, on the Continent, can such utterly indecent exhibitions be daily witnessed as at Margate during bathing hours. Nothing can be more revolting to persons having the least feelings of modesty than the promiscuous mixing of the bathers; nude men dancing, swimming, or floating with women not quite nude, certainly, but with scant clothing. The machines for males and females are not kept apart, and the latter do not apparently care to keep within the awnings. The authorities post notices as to "indecent bathing," but that appears to be all they think they ought to do.

I am, Sir, yours obediently,

B.

To the Editor of " The Times."

SIR,—The account of the scenes which occur at the landing of passengers at the Margate jetty, given by your correspondent to-day, is by no means overcharged. But that is nothing. The rulers of the place seem bent on doing their utmost to keep respectable people away, or, doubtless, long before this the class of visitors would have greatly improved. The sea-fronts of the town, which in the summer would be otherwise enjoyable, are abandoned to the noisy rule of the lowest kinds of itinerant mountebanks, organ-grinders, and niggers; and from early morn till long after nightfall the place is one hopeless, hideous din. There is yet another grievance. The whole of the drainage is discharged upon the rocks to the east of the harbour, considerably above low-water mark; and to the west, where much building is contemplated, drains have already been laid into the sea, and, when these new houses are built and inhabited, bathing at Margate, now its greatest attraction, must cease for ever.

Yours obediently,

Margate, August 18.   PHAROS.

I have printed these letters for several reasons. In the first place, read after them this account of the town of Margate, given in the 'Encyclopædia Britannica,' in 1797: "Margate, a seaport town of Kent, on the north side of the Isle of Thanet, near the North Foreland. It is noted for shipping vast quantities of corn (most, if not all, the product of that island) for London, and has a salt-water bath at the Post-house, which has performed great cures in nervous and paralytic cases."

Now this Isle of Thanet, please to observe, which is an elevated (200 to 400 feet) mass of chalk, separated from the rest of Kent by little rivers and marshy lands, ought to be respected by you (as Englishmen), because it was the first bit of ground ever possessed in this greater island by your Saxon ancestors, when they came over, some six or seven hundred of them only, in three ships, and contented themselves for a while with no more territory than that white island. Also, the North Foreland, you ought, I think, to know, is taken for the terminal point of the two sides of Britain, east and south, in the first geographical account of our dwelling-place, definitely given by a learned person. But you ought, beyond all question, to know, that the cures of the nervous and paralytic cases, attributed seventy years ago to the " salt-water bath at the Post-house," were much more probably to be laid to account of the freshest and changefullest sea-air to be breathed in England, bending the rich corn over that white dry ground, and giving to sight, above the northern and eastern sweep of sea, the loveliest skies that can be seen, not in England only, but perhaps in all the world ; able at least, to challenge the fairest in Europe, to the far south of Italy.

So it was said, I doubt not rightly, by the man who of all others knew best ; the once in five hundred years given painter, whose chief work, as separate from others, was the painting of skies. He knew the colours of the clouds over the sea, from the Bay of Naples to the Hebrides ; and being once asked where, in Europe, were to be . seen the loveliest skies, answered instantly, " In the Isle of Thanet." Where, therefore, and in this very town of Margate, he lived, when he chose to be quit of London, and yet not to travel.

And I can myself give this much confirmatory evidence of his saying ;—that though I never stay in Thanet, the two loveliest skies I have myself ever seen (and next to Turner, I suppose few men of fifty have kept record of so many), were, one at Boulogne, and the other at Abbeville ; that is to say, in precisely the correspondent French districts of corn-bearing chalk, on the other side of the Channel.

"And what are pretty skies to us?" perhaps you will ask me: "or what have they to do with the behaviour of that crowd on Margate Pier?"

Well, my friends, the final result of the education I want you to give your children will be, in a few words, this. They will know what it is to see the sky. They will know what it is to breathe it. And they will know, best of all, what it is to behave under it, as in the presence of a Father who is in heaven.

Faithfully yours,

J. RUSKIN.

FORS CLAVIGERA.

LETTER THE 10th.

THE BARON'S GATE.

DENMARK HILL,

7th September, 1871.

MY FRIENDS,

For the last two or three days, the papers have been full of articles on a speech of Lord Derby's, which, it seems, has set the public mind on considering the land question. My own mind having long ago been both set, and entirely made up, on that question, I have read neither the speech nor the articles on it; but my eye being caught this morning, fortunately, by the words "Doomsday Book" in my 'Daily Telegraph,' and presently looking up the column, by "stalwart arms and heroic souls of free resolute Englishmen," I glanced down the space between, and found this, to me, remarkable passage:

"The upshot is, that, looking at the question from a purely mechanical point of view, we should seek the *beau idéal* in a landowner cultivating huge farms for himself, with abundant machinery and a few well-paid labourers - to manage the mechanism, or delegating the task to the smallest possible number of tenants with capital.   But when we bear in mind the origin of landlordism, of our national needs, and the real interests of the great body of English tenantry, we see how advisable it is to retain intelligent yeomen as part of our means of cultivating the soil."

This is all, then, is it, that your Liberal paper ventures to say for you?   It is *advisable* to retain a *few* intelligent yeomen in the island.   I don't mean to find fault with the ' Daily Telegraph ' : I think it always means well on the whole, and deals fairly ; which is more than can be said for its highly toned and delicately perfumed oppo-nent, the ' Pall Mall Gazette.'   But I think a " Liberal " paper might have said more for the " stalwart arms and heroic souls" than this.   I am going myself to say a great deal more for them, though I am not a Liberal— quite the polar contrary of that.

You, perhaps, have been provoked, in the course of these letters, by not being able to make out *what* I was. It is time you should know, and I will tell you plainly. I am, and my father was before me, a violent Tory of the old school ; (Walter Scott's school, that is to say, and Homer's) I name these two out of the numberless great Tory writers, because they were my own two masters.   I had Walter Scott's novels, and the Iliad, (Pope's translation), for my only reading when I was a child, on week-days : on Sundays their effect was

tempered by 'Robinson Crusoe' and the ' Pilgrim's Progress'; my mother having it deeply in her heart to make
an evangelical clergyman of me.   Fortunately, I had an
aunt more evangelical than my mother ; and my aunt
gave me cold mutton for Sunday's dinner, which—as I
much preferred it hot—greatly diminished the influence
of the ' Pilgrim's Progress,' and the end of the matter
was, that I got all the noble imaginative teaching of
Defoe and Bunyan, and yet—am not an evangelical
clergyman.

I had, however, still better teaching than theirs, and
that compulsorily, and every day of the week.   (Have
patience with me in this egotism ; it is necessary for
many reasons that you should know what influences have
brought me into the temper in which I write to you.)

Walter Scott and Pope's Homer were reading of my
own election, but my mother forced me, by steady daily
toil, to learn long chapters of the Bible by heart; as
well as to read it every syllable through, aloud, hard
names and all, from Genesis to the Apocalypse, about
once a year; and to that discipline—patient, accurate,
and resolute—I owe not only a knowledge of the book,
which I find occasionally serviceable, but much of my
general power of taking pains, and the best part of my
taste in literature.   From Walter Scott's novels I might
easily, as I grew older, have fallen to other people's
novels; and Pope might, perhaps, have led me to take
Johnson's English, or Gibbon's, as types of language ;

but, once knowing the 32nd of Deuteronomy, the 119th
Psalm, the 15th of 1st Corinthians, the Sermon on the
Mount, and most of the Apocalypse, every syllable by
heart, and having always a way of thinking with myself
what words meant, it was not possible for me, even in
the foolishest times of youth, to write entirely super-
ficial or formal English, and the affectation of trying to
write like Hooker and George Herbert was the most
innocent I could have fallen into.

From my own masters, then, Scott and Homer, I
learned the Toryism which my best after-thought has
only served to confirm.

That is to say a most sincere love of kings, and dislike
of everybody who attempted to disobey them. Only, both
by Homer and Scott, I was taught strange ideas about
kings, which I find, for the present, much obsolete ; for,
I perceived that both the author of the Iliad and the
author of Waverley made their kings, or king-loving
persons, do harder work than anybody else. Tydides
or Idomeneus always killed twenty Trojans to other
people's one, and Redgauntlet speared more salmon than
any of the Solway fishermen, and—which was particularly a subject of admiration to me,—I observed that
they not only did more, but in proportion to their
doings, got less, than other people—nay, that the best
of them were even ready to govern for nothing, and let
their followers divide any quantity of spoil or profit. Of
late it has seemed to me that the idea of a king has

become exactly the contrary of this, and that it has been supposed the duty of superior persons generally to do less, and to get more than anybody else ; so that it was, perhaps, quite as well that in those early days my contemplation of existent kingship was a very distant one, and my childish eyes wholly unacquainted with the splendour of courts.

The aunt who gave me cold mutton on Sundays was my father's sister : she lived at Bridge-end, in the town of Perth, and had a garden full of gooseberry-bushes, sloping down to the Tay, with a door opening to the water, which ran past it clear-brown over the pebbles three or four feet deep ; an infinite thing for a child to look down into.

My father began business as a wine-merchant, with no capital, and a considerable amount of debts bequeathed him by my grandfather. He accepted the bequest, and paid them all before he began to lay by anything for himself, for which his best friends called him a fool, and I, without expressing any opinion as to his wisdom, which I knew in such matters to be at least equal to mine, have written on the granite slab over his grave that he was "an entirely honest merchant." As days went on he was able to take a house in Hunter Street, Brunswick Square, No. 54 (the windows of it, fortu-nately for me, commanded a view of a marvellous iron post, out of which the water-carts were filled through beautiful little trap-doors, by pipes like boa-constrictors ;

and I was never weary of contemplating that mystery,
and the delicious dripping consequent); and as years
went on, and I came to be four or five years old, he
could command a postchaise and pair for two months
in the summer, by help of which, with my mother and
me, he went the round of his country customers (who
liked to see the principal of the house his own traveller);
so that, at a jog-trot pace, and through the panoramic
opening of the four windows of a postchaise, made more
panoramic still to me because my seat was a little
bracket in front, (for we used to hire the chaise regularly
for the two months out of Long Acre, and so could have
it bracketed and pocketed as we liked), I saw all the
highroads, and most of the cross ones, of England and
Wales, and great part of lowland Scotland, as far as
Perth, where every other year we spent the whole
summer; and I used to read the 'Abbot' at Kinross,
and the 'Monastery' in Glen Farg, which I confused
with "Glendearg," and thought that the White Lady
had as certainly lived by the streamlet in that glen of
the Ochils, as the Queen of Scots in the island of Loch
Leven.

It happened also, which was the real cause of the
bias of my after life, that my father had a rare love of
pictures. I use the word "rare" advisedly, having never
met with another instance of so innate a faculty for the
discernment of true art, up to the point possible without
actual practice. Accordingly, wherever there was a gallery

to be seen, we stopped at the nearest town for the night; and in reverentest manner I thus saw nearly all the noblemen's houses in England; not indeed myself at that age caring for the pictures, but much for castles and ruins, feeling more and more, as I grew older, the healthy delight of uncovetous admiration, and perceiving, as soon as I could perceive any political truth at all, that it was probably much happier to live in a small house, and have Warwick Castle to be astonished at, than to live in Warwick Castle, and have nothing to be astonished at; but that, at all events, it would not make Brunswick Square in the least more pleasantly habitable, to pull Warwick Castle down. And, at this day, though I have kind invitations enough to visit America, I could not, even for a couple of months, live in a country so miserable as to possess no castles.

Nevertheless, having formed my notion of kinghood chiefly from the FitzJames of the 'Lady of the Lake,' and of noblesse from the Douglas there, and the Douglas in 'Marmion,' a painful wonder soon arose in my child-mind, why the castles should now be always empty. Tantallon was there; but no Archibald of Angus:—Stirling, but no Knight of Snowdoun. The galleries and gardens of England were beautiful to see—but his Lordship and her Ladyship were always in town, said the housekeepers and gardeners. Deep yearning took hold of me for a kind of "Restoration," which I began slowly to feel that Charles the Second had not altogether effected, though

I always wore a gilded oak-apple very reverently in my button-hole on the 29th of May. It seemed to me that Charles the Second's Restoration had been, as compared with the Restoration I wanted, much as that gilded oak-apple to a real apple. And as I grew older, the desire for red pippins instead of brown ones, and Living Kings instead of dead ones, appeared to me rational as well as romantic ; and gradually it has become the main purpose of my life to grow pippins, and its chief hope, to see Kings.

Hope, this last, for others much more than for myself. I can always behave as if I had a King, whether I have one or not ; but it is otherwise with some unfortunate persons. Nothing has ever impressed me so much with the power of kingship, and the need of it, as the declamation of the French Republicans against the Emperor before his fall.

He did not, indeed, meet my old Tory notion of a King ; and in my own business of architecture he was doing, I saw, nothing but mischief ; pulling down lovely buildings, and putting up frightful ones carved all over with L. N.'s : but the intense need of France for a governor of some kind was made chiefly evident to me by the way the Republicans confessed themselves paralyzed by him. Nothing could be done in France, it seemed, because of the Emperor : they could not drive an honest trade ; they could not keep their houses in order ; they could not study the sun and moon ; they could not eat a comfortable déjeûner à la fourchette ; they could not sail in the Gulf of Lyons, nor climb on the Mont d'Or ; they could not, in fine, (so they said,) so much as walk straight, nor speak plain, because of the Emperor. On this side of the water, moreover, the Republicans were all in the same tale. Their opinions, it appeared, were not printed to their minds in the Paris journals, and the world must come to an end therefore. So that, in fact, here was all the Republican force of France and England, confessing itself paralyzed, not so much by a real King, as by the shadow of one. All the harm the extant and visible King did was, to encourage the dressmakers and stone-masons in Paris,—to pay some idle people very large salaries,—and to make some, perhaps agreeably talkative, people, hold their tongues. That, I repeat, was all the harm he did, or could do ; he corrupted nothing but what was voluntarily corruptible,—crushed nothing but what was essentially not solid : and it remained open to these Republican gentlemen to do anything they chose that was useful to France, or honourable to themselves, between earth and heaven, except only—print violent abuse of this shortish man, with a long nose, who stood, as they would have it, between them and heaven. But there they stood, spell-bound ; the one thing suggesting itself to their frantic impotence as feasible, being to get this one shortish man assassinated. Their children would not grow, their corn would not ripen, and the stars would not roll, till they had got this one short man blown into shorter pieces.

If the shadow of a King can thus hold (how many?) millions of men, by their own confession, helpless for terror of it, what power must there be in the substance of one?

But this mass of republicans—vociferous, terrified, and mischievous—is the least part, as it is the vilest, of the great European populace who are lost for want of true kings. It is not these who stand idle, gibbering at a shadow, whom we have to mourn over;—they would have been good for little, even governed;—but those who work and do *not* gibber,—the quiet peasants in the fields of Europe, sad-browed, honest-hearted, full of natural tenderness and courtesy, who have none to help them, and none to teach; who have no kings, except those who rob them while they live, no tutors, except those who teach them—how to die.

I had an impatient remonstrance sent me the other day, by a country clergyman's wife, against that saying in my former letter, " Dying has been more expensive to you than living." Did I know, she asked, what a country clergyman's life was, and that he was the poor man's only friend?

Alas, I know it, and too well. What can be said of more deadly and ghastly blame against the clergy of England, or any other country, than that they are the poor man's only friends?

Have they, then, so betrayed their Master's charge

and mind, in their preaching to the rich ; so smoothed
their words, and so sold their authority,—that, after
twelve hundred years' entrusting of the gospel to them,
there is no man in England (this is their chief plea for
themselves forsooth) who will have mercy on the poor,
but they ; and so they must leave the word of God,
and serve tables ?

I would not myself have said so much against
English clergymen, whether of country or town. Three
—and one dead makes four—of my dear friends (and
I have not many dear friends) are country clergymen ;
and I know the ways of every sort of them ; my archi-
tectural tastes necessarily bringing me into near relations
with the sort who like pointed arches and painted
glass ; and my old religious breeding having given me
an unconquerable habit of taking up with any travelling
tinker of evangelical principles I may come across ;
and even of reading, not without awe, the prophetic
warnings of any persons belonging to that peculiarly
well-informed " persuasion," such, for instance, as those
of Mr. Zion Ward " concerning the fall of Lucifer, in a
letter to a friend, Mr. William Dick, of Glasgow, price
twopence," in which I read (as aforesaid, with unfeigned
feelings of concern,) that " the slain of the Lord shall
be MAN-Y ; that is, man, in whom death is, with all
the works of carnality, shall be burnt up ! "

But I was not thinking either of English clergy, or
of any other group of clergy, specially, when I wrote

that sentence ; but of the entire Clerkly or Learned
Company, from the first priest of Egypt to the last
ordained Belgravian curate, and of all the talk they
have talked, and all the quarrelling they have caused,
and all the gold they have had given them, to this
day, when still " they are the poor man's only friends "
—and by no means all of them that, heartily ! though
I see the Bishop of Manchester has, of late, been
superintending—I beg his pardon, Bishops don't super-
intend—looking on, or over, I should have said—the
recreations of his flock at the seaside ; and " the
thought struck him " that railroads were an advantage
to them in taking them for their holiday out of Manchester. The thought may, perhaps, strike him, next,
that a working man ought to be able to find " holy
days " *in* his home, as well as out of it.*

A year or two ago, a man who had at the time, and
has still, important official authority over much of the
business of the country, was speaking anxiously to me of
the misery increasing in the suburbs and back streets of
London, and debating, with the good help of the Oxford
Regius Professor of Medicine—who was second in council
—what sanitary or moral remedy could be found. The
debate languished, however, because of the strong conviction in the minds of all three of us that the misery
was inevitable in the suburbs of so vast a city. At last,

---

* See § 159, (written seven years ago.) in ‘ Munera Pulveris.’

either the minister or physician, I forget which, expressed the conviction. " Well," I answered, " then you must not have large cities." " That," answered the minister, " is an unpractical saying—you know we *must* have them, under existing circumstances."

I made no reply, feeling that it was vain to assure any man actively concerned in modern parliamentary business, that no measures were " practical " except. those which touched the source of the evil opposed. All systems of government—all efforts of benevolence, are vain to repress the natural consequences of radical error. But any man of influence who had the sense and courage to refuse himself and his family one London season—to stay on his estate, and employ the shopkeepers in his own village, instead of those in Bond Street—would be " practically " dealing with, and conquering, this evil, so far as in him lay ; and contributing with his whole might to the thorough and final conquest of it.

Not but that I know how to meet it directly also, if any London landlords choose so to attack it. You are beginning to hear something of what Miss Hill has done in Marylebone, and of the change brought about by her energy and good sense in the centre of one of the worst districts of London. It is difficult enough, I admit, to find a woman of average sense and tenderness enough to be able for such work ; but there are, indeed, other such in the world, only three-fourths of them now get lost in pious lecturing, or altar-cloth sewing ;

and the wisest remaining fourth stay at home as quiet
house-wives, not seeing their way to wider action ;
nevertheless, any London landlord who will content
himself with moderate and fixed rent, (I get five per cent.
from Miss Hill, which is surely enough !), assuring his
tenants of secure possession if that is paid, so that they
need not fear having their rent raised, if they improve
their houses ; and who will secure also a quiet bit of
ground for their children to play in, instead of the
street,—has established all the necessary conditions of
success ; and I doubt not that Miss Hill herself could
find co-workers able to extend the system of management she has originated, and shown to be so effective.

But the best that can be done in this way will be
useless ultimately, unless the deep source of the misery
be cut off. While Miss Hill, with intense effort and
noble power, has partially moralized a couple of acres
in Marylebone, at least fifty square miles of lovely
country have been Demoralized outside London, by the
increasing itch of the upper classes to live where they
can get some gossip in their idleness, and show each
other their dresses.

That life of theirs must come to an end soon, both
here and in Paris, but to what end, it is, I trust, in
their own power still to decide. If they resolve to
maintain to the last the present system of spending the
rent taken from the rural districts in the dissipation of
the capitals, they will not always find they can secure

a quiet time, as the other day in Dublin, by with-
drawing the police, nor that park-railings are the only
thing which (police being duly withdrawn) will go down.
Those favourite castle battlements of mine, their internal
" police " withdrawn, will go down also ; and I should be
sorry to see it ;—the lords and ladies, houseless at least
in shooting season, perhaps sorrier, though they *did* find
the grey turrets dismal in winter time. If they would
yet have them for autumn, they must have them for
winter. Consider, fair lords and ladies, by the time you
marry, and choose your dwelling-places, there are for
you but forty or fifty winters more in whose dark days
you may see the snow fall and wreathe. There will be
no snow in Heaven, I presume—still less elsewhere, (if
lords and ladies ever miss of Heaven).

And that some may, is perhaps conceivable, for there
are more than a few things to be managed on an
English estate, and to be " faithful " in those few
cannot be interpreted as merely abstracting the rent
of them. Nay, even the Telegraph's beau ideal of the
landowner, from a mechanical point of view, may come
short, somewhat. " Cultivating huge farms for himself
with abundant machinery ;—" Is that Lord Derby's
ideal also, may it be asked ? The Scott-reading of
my youth haunts me, and I seem still listening to the
(perhaps a little too long) speeches of the Black Countess
who appears terrifically through the sliding panel in
' Peveril of the Peak,' about " her sainted Derby." Would

Saint Derby's ideal, or his Black Countess's, of due ordinance for their castle and estate of Man, have been a minimum of Man therein, and an abundance of machinery? In fact, only the Trinacrian Legs of Man, transposed into many spokes of wheels—no use for "stalwart arms" any more—and less than none for inconveniently "heroic" souls?

"Cultivating huge farms for himself!" I don't even see, after the sincerest efforts to put myself into a mechanical point of view, how it is to be done. For himself? Is he to eat the cornricks then? Surely such a beau ideal is more Utopian than any of mine? Indeed, whether it be praise or blame-worthy, it is not so easy to cultivate anything wholly for oneself, nor to consume, oneself, the products of cultivation. I have, indeed, before now, hinted to you that perhaps the "consumer" was not so necessary a person economically, as has been supposed ; nevertheless, it is not in his own mere eating and drinking, or even his picture-collecting, that a false lord injures the poor. It is in his bidding and forbidding—or worse still, in ceasing to do either. I have given you another of Giotto's pictures, this month, his imagination of Injustice, which he has seen done in his time, as we in ours ; and I am sorry to observe that his Injustice lives in a battlemented castle and in a mountain country, it appears ; the gates of it between rocks, and in the midst of a wood ; but in Giotto's time, woods were too many, and towns too few. Also, Injustice has indeed very ugly talons to his fingers, like Envy ; and an ugly quadruple hook to his lance, and other ominous resemblances to the " hooked bird," the falcon, which both knights and ladies too much delighted in. Nevertheless Giotto's main idea about him is, clearly, that he " sits in the gate " pacifically, with a cloak thrown over his chain-armour (you can just see the links of it appear at his throat), and a plain citizen's cap for a helmet, and his sword sheathed, while all robbery and violence have way in the wild places round him,—he heedless.

Which is, indeed, the depth of Injustice : not the harm you do, but that you permit to be done,—hooking perhaps here and there something to you with your clawed weapon meanwhile. The baronial type exists still, I fear, in such manner, here and there, in spite of improving centuries.

My friends, we have been thinking, perhaps, to-day, more than we ought of our masters' faults,—scarcely enough of our own. If you would have the upper classes do *their* duty, see that you also do yours. See that you can obey good laws, and good lords, or law-wards, if you once get them—that you believe in goodness enough to know what a good law is. A good law is one that holds, whether you recognize and pronounce it or not ; a bad law is one that cannot hold, however much you ordain and pronounce it. That is the mighty truth which Carlyle has been telling you for a quarter of a century—once for all he told it you, and the land-

owners, and all whom it concerns, in the third book of
' Past and Present' (1845, buy Chapman and Hall's second
edition if you can, it is good print, and read it till you
know it by heart), and from that day to this, whatever
there is in England of dullest and insolentest may be
always known by the natural instinct it has to howl
against Carlyle. Of late, matters coming more and
more to crisis, the liberty men seeing their way, as they
think, more and more broad and bright before them,
and still this too legible and steady old sign-post saying,
That it is *not* the way, lovely as it looks, the outcry
against it becomes deafening. Now, I tell you once for
all, Carlyle is the only living writer who has spoken the
absolute and perpetual truth about yourselves and your
business; and exactly in proportion to the inherent
weakness of brain in your lying guides, will be their
animosity against Carlyle. Your lying guides, observe,
I say—not meaning that they lie wilfully—but that their
nature is to do nothing else. For in the modern Liberal
there is a new and wonderful form of misguidance. Of
old, it was bad enough that the blind should lead the
blind; still, with dog and stick, or even timid walking
with recognized need of dog and stick, if not to be had,
such leadership might come to good end enough; but
now a worse disorder has come upon you, that the
squinting should lead the squinting. Now the nature
of bat, or mole, or owl, may be undesirable, at least in
the day-time, but worse may be imagined. The modern

Liberal politico-economist of the Stuart Mill school is essentially of the type of a flat-fish—one eyeless side of him always in the mud, and one eye, on the side that *has* eyes, down in the corner of his mouth,—not a desirable guide for man or beast. There was an article —I believe it got in by mistake, but the Editor, of course, won't say so—in the 'Contemporary Review,' two months back, on Mr. Morley's Essays, by a Mr. Buchanan, with an incidental page on Carlyle in it, unmatchable (to the length of my poor knowledge) for obliquitous platitude in the mud-walks of literature.

Read your Carlyle, then, with all your heart, and with the best of brain you can give ; and you will learn from him first, the eternity of good law, and the need of obedience to it : then, concerning your own immediate business, you will learn farther this, that the beginning of all good law, and nearly the end of it, is in these two ordinances,—That every man shall do good work for his bread : and secondly, that every man shall have good bread for his work. But the first of these is the only one you have to think of. If you are resolved that the work shall be good, the bread will be sure ; if not,—believe me, there is neither steam plough nor steam mill, go they never so glibly, that will win it from the earth long, either for you, or the Ideal Landed Proprietor.

Faithfully yours,

J. RUSKIN.

FORS CLAVIGERA.

LETTER THE 11th.

THE ABBOT'S CHAPEL.

DENMARK HILL,
15*th October*, 1871.

MY FRIENDS,

A day seldom passes, now that people begin to notice these Letters a little, without my receiving a remonstrance on the absurdity of writing "so much above the level" of those whom I address.

I have said, however, that eventually you shall understand, if you care to understand, every word in these pages. Through all this year I have only been putting questions; some of them such as have puzzled the wisest, and which may, for a long time yet, prove too hard for you and me: but, next year, I will go over all the ground again, answering the questions, where I know of any answers; or making them plain for your examination, when I know of none.

But, in the meantime, be it admitted, for argument's sake, that this way of writing, which is easy to me, and which most educated persons can easily understand, *is*

very much above your level. I want to know why it is
assumed so quietly that your brains must always be at
a low level? Is it essential to the doing of the work
by which England exists, that its workmen should not
be able to understand scholar's English, (remember, I
only assume mine to be so for argument's sake), but only
newspaper's English? I chanced, indeed, to take up a
number of ' Belgravia ' the other day, which contained a
violent attack on an old enemy of mine—' Blackwood's
Magazine '; and I enjoyed the attack mightily, until
' Belgravia ' declared, by way of coup-de-grace to ' Blackwood,' that something which ' Blackwood ' had spoken
of as settled in one way had been irrevocably settled
the other way,—"settled," said triumphant ' Belgravia,'
" in seventy-two newspapers."

Seventy-two newspapers, then, it seems—or, with a
margin, eighty-two,—perhaps, to be perfectly safe, we
had better say ninety-two—are enough to settle anything in this England of ours, for the present. But,
irrevocably, I doubt. If, perchance, you workmen
should reach the level of understanding scholar's English
instead of newspaper's English, things might a little
unsettle themselves again ; and, in the end, might even
get into positions uncontemplated by the ninety-two
newspapers,—contemplated only by the laws of Heaven,
and settled by them, some time since, as positions which,
if things ever got out of, they would need to get into
again.

And, for my own part, I cannot at all understand why well-educated people should still so habitually speak of you as beneath their level, and needing to be written down to, with condescending simplicity, as flat-foreheaded creatures of another race, unredeemable by any Darwinism.

I was waiting last Saturday afternoon on the platform of the railway station at Furness Abbey; (the station itself is tastefully placed so that you can see it, and nothing else but it, through the east window of the Abbot's Chapel, over the ruined altar;) and a party of the workmen employed on another line, wanted for the swiftly progressive neighbourhood of Dalton, were taking Sabbatical refreshment at the tavern recently established at the south side of the said Abbot's Chapel. Presently, the train whistling for them, they came out in a highly refreshed state, and made for it as fast as they could by the tunnel under the line, taking very long steps to keep their balance in the direction of motion, and securing themselves, laterally, by hustling the wall, or any chance passengers. They were dressed universally in brown rags, which, perhaps, they felt to be the comfortablest kind of dress; they had, most of them, pipes, which I really believe to be more enjoyable than cigars; they got themselves adjusted in their carriages by the aid of snatches of vocal music, and looked at us,—(I had charge of a lady and her two young daughters),—with supreme indifference, as indeed at creatures of another

race ; pitiable, perhaps,—certainly disagreeable and ob-
jectionable—but, on the whole, despicable, and not to
be minded. We, on our part, had the insolence to pity
them for being dressed in rags, and for being packed
so close in the third-class carriages : the two young
girls bore being run against patiently ; and when a
thin boy of fourteen or fifteen, the most drunk of the
company, was sent back staggering to the tavern for a
forgotten pickaxe, we would, any of us, I am sure, have
gone and fetched it for him, if he had asked us. For we
were all in a very virtuous and charitable temper : we
had had an excellent dinner at the new inn, and had
earned that portion of our daily bread by admiring
the Abbey all the morning. So we pitied the poor
workmen doubly—first, for being so wicked as to get
drunk at four in the afternoon ; and, secondly, for being
employed in work so disgraceful as throwing up clods
of earth into an embankment, instead of spending the
day, like us, in admiring the Abbey : and I, who am
always making myself a nuisance to people with my
political economy, inquired timidly of my friend whether
she thought it all quite right. And she said, certainly
not ; but what could be done ? It was of no use trying
to make such men admire the Abbey, or to keep them
from getting drunk. They wouldn't do the one, and they
would do the other—they were quite an unmanageable
sort of people, and had been so for generations.

Which, indeed, I knew to be partly the truth, but it

only made the thing seem to me more wrong than it did
before, since here were not only the actual two or three
dozen of unmanageable persons, with much taste for beer,
and none for architecture ; but these implied the existence
of many unmanageable persons before and after them,—
nay, a long ancestral and filial unmanageableness. They
were a Fallen Race, every way incapable, as I acutely
felt, of appreciating the beauty of ' Modern Painters,'
or fathoming the significance of ' Fors Clavigera.'

But what they had done to deserve their fall, or what
I had done to deserve the privilege of being the author
of those valuable books, remained obscure to me ; and
indeed, whatever the deservings may have been on either
side, in this and other cases of the kind, it is always a
marvel to me that the arrangement and its consequences
are accepted so patiently. For observe what, in brief
terms, the arrangement is. Virtually, the entire business
of the world turns on the clear necessity of getting on
table, hot or cold, if possible, meat—but, at least, vegetables,—at some hour of the day, for all of us : for you
labourers, we will say at noon ; for us æsthetical persons, we will say at eight in the evening ; for we like
to have done our eight hours' work of admiring abbeys
before we dine. But, at some time of day, the mutton
and turnips, or, since mutton itself is only a transformed
state of turnips, we may say, as sufficiently typical of
everything, turnips only, must absolutely be got for us
both. And nearly every problem of State policy and

economy, as at present understood, and practised, consists in some device for persuading you labourers to go
and dig up dinner for us reflective and æsthetical
persons, who like to sit still, and think, or admire.   So
that when we get to the bottom of the matter, we find
the inhabitants of this earth broadly divided into two
great masses ;—the peasant paymasters—spade in hand,
original and imperial producers of turnips ; and, waiting
on them all round, a crowd of polite persons, modestly
expectant of turnips, for some—too often theoretical—
service.   There is, first, the clerical person, whom the
peasant pays in turnips for giving him moral advice ;
then the legal person, whom the peasant pays in turnips
for telling him, in black letter, that his house is his
own ; there is, thirdly, the courtly person, whom the
peasant pays in turnips for presenting a celestial appearance to him ; there is, fourthly, the literary person, whom
the peasant pays in turnips for talking daintily to him ;
and there is, lastly, the military person, whom the
peasant pays in turnips for standing, with a cocked hat
on, in the middle of the field, and exercising a moral
influence upon the neighbours.   Nor is the peasant to
be pitied if these arrangements are all faithfully carried
out.   If he really gets moral advice from his moral
adviser ; if his house is, indeed, maintained to be his
own, by his legal adviser ; if courtly persons, indeed,
present a celestial appearance to him ; and literary
persons, indeed, talk beautiful words : if, finally, his

scarecrow do, indeed, stand quiet, as with a stick through the middle of it, producing, if not always a wholesome terror, at least, a picturesque effect, and colour-contrast of scarlet with green,—they are all of them worth their daily turnips. But if, perchance, it happen that he get *im*moral advice from his moralist, or if his lawyer advise him that his house is *not* his own ; and his bard, story-teller, or other literary charmer, begin to charm him unwisely, not with beautiful words, but with obscene and ugly words—and he be readier with his response in vegetable produce for these than for any other sort ; finally, if his quiet scarecrow become disquiet, and seem likely to bring upon him a whole flight of scarecrows out of his neighbours' fields,—the combined fleets of Russia, Prussia, etc., as my friend and your trustee, Mr. Cowper-Temple, has it, (see above, Letter II., p. 21,) it is time to look into such arrangements under their several heads.

Well looked after, however, all these arrangements have their advantages, and a certain basis of reason and propriety. But there are two other arrangements which have no basis on either, and which are very widely adopted, nevertheless, among mankind, to their great misery.

I must expand a little the type of my primitive peasant before defining these. You observe, I have not named among the polite persons giving theoretical service in exchange for vegetable diet, the large, and lately become exceedingly polite, class, of artists. For a true artist is only a beautiful development of tailor or carpenter. As the peasant provides the dinner, so the artist provides the clothes and house : in the tailoring and tapestry producing function, the best of artists ought to be the peasant's wife herself, when properly emulative of Queens Penelope, Bertha, and Maude ; and in the house-producing-and-painting function, though concluding itself in such painted chambers as those of the Vatican, the artist is still typically and essentially a carpenter or mason ; first carving wood and stone, then painting the same for preservation ;—if ornamentally, all the better. And, accordingly, you see these letters of mine are addressed to the " workmen and labourers " of England,—that is to say, to the providers of houses and dinners, for themselves, and for all men, in this country, as in all others.

Considering these two sorts of Providers, then, as one great class, surrounded by the suppliant persons for whom, together with themselves, they have to make provision, it is evident that they both have need originally of two things—land, and tools. Clay to be subdued ; and plough, or potter's wheel, wherewith to subdue it.

Now, as aforesaid, so long as the polite surrounding personages are content to offer their salutary advice, their legal information, etc., to the peasant, for what these articles are verily worth in vegetable produce, all is perfectly fair ; but if any of the polite persons contrive to get hold of the peasant's land, or of his tools, and put him into the " position of William," and make him pay annual interest, first for the wood that he planes, and then for the plane he planes it with !—my friends, polite or otherwise, these two arrangements cannot be considered as settled yet, even by the ninety-two newspapers, with all Belgravia to back them.

Not by the newspapers, nor by Belgravia, nor even by the Cambridge Catechism, or the Cambridge Professor of Political Economy.

Look to the beginning of the second chapter in the last edition of Professor Fawcett's Manual of Political Economy, (Macmillan, 1869, p. 105). The chapter purports to treat of the " Classes among whom wealth is distributed." And thus it begins :—

We have described the requisites of production to be three : land, labour, and capital. Since, therefore, land, labour, and capital are essential to the production of wealth, it is natural to suppose that the wealth which is produced ought to be possessed by those who own the land, labour, and capital which have respectively contributed to its production. The share of wealth which is thus allotted to the possessor of the land is termed rent ; the portion allotted to the labourer is termed wages, and the remuneration of the capitalist is termed profit.

You observe that in this very meritoriously clear sentence both the possessor of the land and the possessor of the capital are assumed to be absolutely idle persons. If they contributed any labour to the business, and so confused themselves with the labourer, the problem of triple division would become complicated directly ;—in point of fact, they do occasionally employ themselves somewhat, and become deserving, therefore, of a share, not of rent only, nor of profit only, but of wages also. And every now and then, as I noted in my last letter, there is an outburst of admiration in some one of the ninety-two newspapers, at the amount of " work " done by persons of the superior classes ; respecting which, however, you remember that I also advised you that a great deal of it was only a form of competitive play. In the main, therefore, the statement of the **Cam-bridge** Professor may be admitted to be correct as to the existing facts ; the Holders of land and capital being virtually in a state of Dignified Repose, as the Labourer is in a state of—(at least, I hear it always so announced in the ninety-two newspapers)—Dignified Labour.

But Professor Fawcett's sentence, though, as I have just said, in comparison with most writings on the subject, meritoriously clear, yet is not as clear as it might be,— still less as scientific as it might be. It is, indeed, gracefully ornamental, in the use, in its last clause, of the three words, " share," " portion," and " remuneration," for the same thing ; but this is not the clearest imagin- able language. The sentence, strictly put, should run thus :—" The portion of wealth which is thus allotted to the possessor of the land is termed rent ; the portion allotted to the labourer is termed wages ; and the portion allotted to the capitalist is termed profit."

And you may at once see the advantage of reducing the sentence to these more simple terms ; for Professor Fawcett's ornamental language has this danger in it, that " Remuneration," being so much grander a word than " Portion," in the very roll of it seems to imply rather a thousand pounds a day than three-and-sixpence. And until there be scientific reason shown for anticipating the portions to· be thus disproportioned, we have no right to suggest their being so, by ornamental variety of language.

Again, Professor Fawcett's sentence is, I said, not entirely scientific. He founds the entire principle of allotment on the phrase " it is natural to suppose." But I never heard of any other science founded on what it was natural to suppose. Do the Cambridge mathematicians, then, in these advanced days, tell their pupils that it is natural to suppose the three angles of a triangle are equal to two right ones ? Nay, in the present case, I regret to say it has sometimes been thought wholly *un*natural to suppose any such thing ; and so exceedingly unnatural, that to receive either a " remuneration," or a " portion," or a " share," for the loan of anything, without personally working, was held by Dante and other such simple persons in the Middle Ages to

be one of the worst of the sins that could be committed
against nature : and the receivers of such interest were
put in the same circle of Hell with the people of Sodom
and Gomorrah.

'And it is greatly to be apprehended that if ever
our workmen, under the influences of Mr. · Scott and
Mr. Street, come indeed to admire the Abbot's Chapel
at Furness more than the railroad station, they may
become possessed of a taste for Gothic opinions as well
as Gothic arches, and think it " natural to suppose " that
a workman's tools should be his own property.

Which I, myself, having been always given to Gothic
opinions, do, indeed suppose, very strongly ; and intend
to 'try with all my might to bring about that arrangement wherever I have any influence ;—the arrangement
itself being feasible enough, if we can only begin by
not leaving our pickaxes behind us after taking Sabbatical refreshment.

But let me again, and yet again, warn you, that
only by beginning so,—that is to say, by doing what is
in your own power to achieve of plain right,—can you ever
bring about any of your wishes ; or, indeed, can you, to
any practical purpose, begin to wish.   Only by quiet and
decent exaltation of your own habits can you qualify
yourselves to discern what is just, or to define even
what is possible.   I hear you are, at last, beginning
to draw up your wishes in a definite manner ; (I chal-
lenged you to do so, in ' Time and Tide,' four years ago,

in vain), and you mean to have them at last "represented in Parliament ;" but I hear of small question yet
among you, whether they be just wishes, and can be
represented to the power of everlasting Justice, as things
not only natural to be supposed, but necessary to be
done. For *she* accepts no representation of things in
beautiful language, but takes her own view of them, with
her own eyes.

I did, indeed, cut out a slip from the ' Birmingham
Morning News,' last September, (12th,) containing a letter
written by a gentleman signing himself "Justice" in
person, and professing himself an engineer, who talked
very grandly about the "individual and social laws of
our nature:" but *he* had arrived at the inconvenient con-
clusions that "no individual has a natural right to hold
property in land," and that "all land sooner or later
must become public property." I call this an inconvenient conclusion, because I really think you would find
yourselves greatly inconvenienced if your wives couldn't
go into the garden to cut a cabbage, without getting
leave from the Lord Mayor and Corporation ; and
if the same principle is to be carried out as regards
tools, I beg to state to Mr. Justice-in-Person, that if
anybody and everybody is to use my own particular
palette and brushes, I resign my office of Professor of
Fine Art. Perhaps, when we become really acquainted
with the true Justice in Person, not professing herself
an engineer, she may suggest to us, as a Natural

Supposition,—" That land should be given to those who can use *it*, and tools to those who can use *them ;* " and I have a notion you will find this a very tenable supposition also.

I have given you, this month, the last of the pictures I want you to see from Padua ;—Giotto's Image of Justice—which, you observe, differs somewhat from the Image of Justice we used to set up in England, above insurance offices, and the like. Bandaged close about the eyes, our English Justice was wont to be, with a pair of grocers' scales in her hand, wherewith, doubt-less, she was accustomed to weigh out accurately their shares to the landlords, and portions to the labourers, and remunerations to the capitalists. But Giotto's Justice has no bandage about her eyes, (Albert Durer's has them *round* open, and flames flashing from them,) and weighs, not with scales, but with her own hands ; and weighs not merely the shares, or remunerations of men, but the worth of them ; and finding them worth this or that, gives them what they deserve—death, or honour. Those are her forms of " Remuneration."

Are you sure that you are ready to accept the decrees of this true goddess, and to be chastised or rewarded by her, as is your due, being seen through and through to your heart's core ? Or will you still abide by the level balance of the blind Justice of old time ; or rather, by the oblique balance of the squinting Justice of our modern geological Mud-Period ?—the mud, at present, becoming also more slippery under the feet—I beg pardon, the belly—of squinting Justice, than was once expected ; becoming, indeed, (as it is announced, even by Mr. W. P. Price, M.P., chairman at the last half-yearly meeting of the Midland Railway Company,) quite "delicate ground."

The said chairman, you will find, by referring to the ' Pall Mall Gazette ' of August 17th, 1871, having received a letter from Mr. Bass on the subject of the length of time that the servants of the company were engaged in labour, and their inadequate remuneration, made the following remarks .—" He (Mr. Bass) is treading on very delicate ground. The remuneration of labour, the value of which, like the value of gold itself, depends altogether on the one great universal law of supply and demand, is a question on which there is very little room for senti-ment. He, as a very successful tradesman, knows very well how much the success of commercial operations depends on the observance of that law ; and we, sitting here as your representatives, cannot altogether close our eyes to it."

Now it is quite worth your while to hunt out that number of the ' Pall Mall Gazette' in any of your free libraries, because a quaint chance in the placing of the type has produced a lateral comment on these remarks of Mr. W. P. Price, M.P.

Take your carpenter's rule, apply it level under the words, "Great Universal Law of Supply and Demand,"

and read the line it marks off in the other column of the same page. It marks off this, "In Khorassan one-third of the whole population has perished from starvation, and at Ispahan no less than 27,000 souls."

Of course you will think it no business of yours if people are starved in Persia. But the Great "Universal" Law of Supply and Demand may some day operate in the same manner over here; and even in the Mud-and-Flat-fish period, John Bull may not like to have his belly flattened for him to that extent.

You have heard it said occasionally that I am not a practical person. It may be satisfactory to you to know, on the contrary, that this whole plan of mine is founded on the very practical notion of making you round persons instead of flat. Round and merry, instead of flat and sulky. And my beau-ideal is not taken from "a mechanical point of view," but is one already realized. I saw last summer, in the flesh, as round and merry a person as I ever desire to see. He was tidily dressed—not in brown rags, but in green velveteen; he wore a jaunty hat, with a feather in it, a little on one side; he was not drunk, but the effer-vescence of his shrewd good-humour filled the room all about him; and he could sing like a robin. You may say "like a nightingale," if you like, but I think robin's singing the best, myself; only I hardly ever hear it now, for the young ladies of England have had nearly all the robins shot, to wear in their hats, and the bird-stuffers are exporting the few remaining to America.

This merry round person was a Tyrolese peasant; and I hold it an entirely practical proceeding, since I find my idea of felicity actually produced in the Tyrol, to set about the production of it, here, on Tyrolese principles; which, you will find, on inquiry, have not hitherto implied the employment of steam, nor submission to the great Universal Law of Supply and Demand, nor even Demand for the Local Supply of a "Liberal" government. But they do imply labour of all hands on pure earth and in fresh air. They do imply obedience to government which endeavours to be moral. And they result in strength of limbs, clearness of throats, roundness of waists, and pretty jackets, and still prettier corsets to fit them.

I must pass, disjointedly, to matters which, in a written letter, would have been put in a postscript; but I do not care, in a printed one, to leave a useless gap in the type. First, the reference in page 11 of last number to the works of Mr. Zion Ward, is incorrect. The passage I quoted is not in the "Letter to a Friend," price twopence, but in the "Origin of Evil Discovered," price fourpence. (John Bolton, Steel House Lane, Birmingham.) And, by the way, I wish that booksellers would save themselves, and me, some (now steadily enlarging) trouble, by noting that the price of these Letters to friends of mine, as supplied by me, the original inditer, to all and sundry, through my only shopman, Mr. Allen, is seven-pence per epistle, and not fivepence half-penny; and that the trade profit on the sale of them is intended to be, and must eventually be, as I intend, a quite honestly confessed profit, charged to the customer, not compressed out of the author; which object may be easily achieved by the retail bookseller, if he will resolvedly charge the symmetrical sum of Tenpence per epistle over his counter, as it is my purpose he should. But to return to Mr. Ward; the correction of my reference was sent me by one of his disciples, in a very earnest and courteous letter, written chiefly to complain that my quotation totally misrepresented Mr. Ward's opinions. I regret that it should have done so, but gave the quotation neither to represent, nor misrepresent Mr. Ward's opinions; but to show, which the sentence, though brief, quite sufficiently shows, that he had no right to have any.

I have before noted to you, indeed, that, in a broad sense, *nobody* has a right to have opinions; but only knowledges: and, in a practical and large sense, nobody has a right even to make experiments, but only to act in a way which they certainly know will be productive of good. And this I ask you to observe again, because I begin now to receive some earnest inquiries respecting the plan I have in hand, the inquiries very naturally assuming it to be an " experiment," which may possibly be successful, and much more possibly may fail. But it is not an experiment at all. It will be merely the carrying out of what has been done already in some places, to the best of my narrow power, in other places: and so far as it can be carried, it *must* be productive of some kind of good.

For example; I have round me here at Denmark Hill seven acres of leasehold ground. I pay £50 a year ground-rent, and £250 a year in wages to my gardeners; besides expenses in fuel for hothouses, and the like. And for this sum of three hundred odd pounds a year I have some pease and strawberries in summer; some camellias and azaleas in winter; and good cream, and a quiet place to walk in, all the year round. Of the strawberries, cream, and pease, I eat more than is good for me; sometimes, of course, obliging my friends with a superfluous pottle or pint. The camellias and azaleas stand in the ante-room of my library; and everybody says, when they come in, "How pretty!" and my young lady friends have leave to gather what they like to put in their hair, when they are going to balls. Meantime, outside of my fenced seven acres—owing to the operation of the great universal law of supply and demand—numbers of people are starving; many more, dying of too much gin; and many of their children dying of too little milk; and, as I told you in my first Letter, for my own part, I won't stand this sort of thing any longer.

Now it is evidently open to me to say to my gardeners,

" I want no more azaleas or camellias ; and no more strawberries and pease than are good for me. Make these seven acres everywhere as productive of good corn, vegetables, or milk, as you can ; I will have no steam used upon them, for nobody on my ground shall be blown to pieces ; nor any fuel wasted in making plants blossom in winter, for I believe we shall, without such unseasonable blossoms, enjoy the spring twice as much as now ; but, in any part of the ground that is not good for eatable vegetables you are to sow such wild flowers as it seems to like, and you are to keep all trim and orderly. The produce of the land, after I have had my limited and salutary portion of pease, shall be your own ; but if you sell any of it, part of the price you get for it, shall be deducted from your wages."

Now observe, there would be no experiment whatever in any one feature of this proceeding. My gardeners might be stimulated to some extra exertion by it ; but in any event I should retain exactly the same command over them that I had before. I might save something out of my £250 of wages, but I should pay no more than I do now, and in return for the gift of the produce I should certainly be able to exact compliance from my people with any such capricious fancies of mine as that they should wear velveteen jackets, or send their children to learn to sing ; and, indeed, I could grind them, generally, under the iron heel of Despotism, as the ninety-two newspapers would declare, to an extent unheard of before in this free country. And, assuredly, some children would get milk, strawberries, and wild flowers who do not get them now ; and my young lady friends would still, I am firm in my belief, look pretty enough at their balls, even without the camellias or azaleas.

I am not going to do this with my seven acres here ; first, because they are only leasehold ; secondly, because they are too near London for wild flowers to grow brightly in. But I have bought, instead, twice as many freehold acres, where wild flowers are growing now, and shall continue to grow ; and there I mean to live ; and, with the tenth part of my available fortune, I will buy other bits of freehold land, and employ gardeners on them in this above-stated matter. I may as well tell you at once that my tithe will be, roughly, about seven thousand pounds altogether, (a little less rather than more). If I get no help, I can show what I mean, even with this ; but if any one cares to help me with gifts of either money or land, they will find that what they give is applied honestly, and does a perfectly definite service : they might, for aught I know, do more good with it in other ways ; but *some* good in this way—and that is all I assert—they will do, certainly, and not experimentally. And the longer they take to think of the matter the better I shall like it, for my work at Oxford is more than enough for me just now, and I shall not practically bestir myself in this land-scheme for a year to come, at least ;

nor then, except as a rest from my main business : but the money and land will always be safe in the hands of your trustees for you, and you need not doubt, though I show no petulant haste about the matter, that I remain

Faithfully yours,

J. RUSKIN.

FORS CLAVIGERA.

LETTER THE 12th.

THE PRINCE'S LESSON.

DENMARK HILL,
23rd December, 1871.

MY FRIENDS,

You will scarcely care to read anything I have
to say to you this evening—having much to think of,
wholly pleasant, as I hope ; and prospect of delightful
days to come next week. At least, however, you will be
glad to know that I have really made you the Christmas
gift I promised—£7,000 Consols, in all, clear ; a fair
tithe of what I had : and to as much perpetuity as
the law will allow me. It will not allow the dead to
have their own way, long, whatever licence it grants the
living in their humours : and this seems to me unkind
to those helpless ones ;—very certainly it is inexpedient
for the survivors. For the wisest men are wise to the
full in death ; and if you would give them, instead of
stately tombs, only so much honour as to do their will,
when they themselves can no more contend for it, you

would find it good memorial of them, such as the best of them would desire, and full of blessing to all men for all time.

English law needs mending in many respects ; in none more than in this.   As it stands, I can only vest my gift in trustees, desiring them, in the case of my death, immediately to appoint their own successors, and in such continued succession, to apply the proceeds of the St. George's Fund to the purchase of land in England and Scotland, which shall be cultivated to the utmost attainable fruitfulness and beauty by the labour of man and beast thereon, such men and beasts receiving at the same time the best education attainable by the trustees for labouring creatures, according to the terms stated in this book, Fors Clavigera.

These terms, and the arrangement of the whole matter, will become clearer to you as you read on with me, and cannot be clear at all, till you do ;—here is the money, at any rate, to help you, one day, to make merry with, only, if you care to give me any thanks, will you pause now for a moment from your merrymaking, to tell me,— to whom, as Fortune has ordered it, no merrymaking is possible at this time, (nor, indeed, much at any time ;)— to me, therefore, standing as it were astonished in the midst of this gaiety of yours, will you tell—what it is all about ?

Your little children would answer, doubtless ,fearlessly, " Because the Child Christ was born to-day :" but you, wiser than your children, it may be,—at least, it should be,—are you also sure that He was?

And if He was, what is that to you?

I repeat, are you indeed *sure* He was? I mean, with real happening of the strange things you have been told, that the Heavens opened near Him, showing their hosts, and that one of their stars stood still over His head? You are sure of that, you say? I am glad; and wish it were so with me; but I have been so puzzled lately by many matters that once seemed clear to me, that I seldom now feel sure of anything. Still seldomer, however, do I feel sure of the contrary of anything. That people say they saw it, may not prove that it was visible; but that I never saw it cannot prove that it was invisible: and this is a story which I more envy the people who believe on the weakest grounds, than who deny on the strongest. The people whom I envy not at all are those who imagine they believe it, and do not.

For one of two things this story of the Nativity *is* certainly, and without any manner of doubt. It relates either a fact full of power, or a dream full of meaning. It is, at the least, not a cunningly devised fable, but the record of an impression made, by some strange spiritual cause, on the minds of the human race, at the most critical period of their existence:—an impression which has produced, in past ages, the greatest effect on mankind ever yet achieved by an intellectual conception; and which is yet to guide, by the determination of its truth or falsehood, the absolute destiny of ages to come.

Will you give some little time therefore, to think of it with me to-day, being, as you tell me, sure of its truth ? What, then, let me ask you, is its truth to *you ?* The Child for whose birth you are rejoicing was born, you are told, to save His people from their sins ; but I have never noticed that you were particularly conscious of any sins to be saved from. If I were to tax you with any one in particular—lying, or thieving, or the like— my belief is you would say directly I had no business to do anything of the kind.

Nay, but, you may perhaps answer me—" That is because we *have* been saved from our sins ; and we are making merry, because we are so perfectly good."

Well ; there would be some reason in such an answer. There is much goodness in you to be thankful for : far more than you know, or have learned to trust. Still, I don't believe you will tell me seriously that you eat your pudding and go to your pantomimes only to express your satisfaction that you are so very good.

What is, or may be, this Nativity, to you, then, I repeat ? Shall we consider, a little, what, at all events, it was to the people of its time ; and so make ourselves more clear as to what it might be to us ? We will read slowly.

" And there were, in that country, shepherds, staying out in the field, keeping watch over their flocks by night."

Watching night and day, that means ; not going home. The staying out in the field is the translation of a word from which a Greek nymph has her name, Agraulos, "the stayer out in fields," of whom I shall have something to tell you soon.

"And behold, the Messenger of the Lord stood above them, and the glory of the Lord lightened round them, and they feared a great fear."

"Messenger." You must remember that, when this was written, the word "angel" had only the effect of our word—"messenger"—on men's minds. Our translators say "angel" when they like, and "messenger" when they like ; but the Bible, messenger only, or angel only, as you please. For instance, "Was not Rahab the harlot justified by works, when she had received the angels, and sent them forth another way ?"

Would not you fain know what this angel looked like ? I have always grievously wanted, from childhood upwards, to know that ; and gleaned diligently every word written by people who said they had seen angels : but none of them ever tell me what their eyes are like, or hair, or even what dress they have on. We dress them, in pictures, conjecturally, in long robes, falling gracefully ; but we only continue to think that kind of dress angelic, because religious young girls, in their modesty, and wish to look only human, give their dresses flounces. When I was a child, I used to be satisfied by hearing that angels had always two wings, and sometimes six; but now nothing dissatisfies me so much as hearing that; for my business compels me continually into close drawing of wings; and now they never give me the notion of anything but a swift or a gannet. And, worse still, when I see a picture of an angel, I know positively where he got his wings from—not at all from any heavenly vision, but from the worshipped hawk and ibis, down through Assyrian flying bulls, and Greek flying horses, and Byzantine flying evangelists, till we get a brass eagle, (of all creatures in the world, to choose!) to have the gospel of peace read from the back of it.

Therefore, do the best I can, no idea of an angel is possible to me. And when I ask my religious friends, they tell me not to wish to be wise above that which is written. My religious friends, let me write a few words of this letter, not to my poor puzzled workmen, but to you, who will all be going serenely to church to-morrow. This messenger, formed as we know not, stood above the shepherds, and the glory of the Lord lightened round them.

You would have liked to have seen it, you think! Brighter than the sun; perhaps twenty-one coloured, instead of seven-coloured, and as bright as the lime-light: doubtless you would have liked to see it, at midnight, in Judæa.

You tell me not to be wise above that which is written; why, therefore, should you be desirous, above that which is given? You cannot see the glory of God as bright as the lime-light at midnight ; but you may see it as bright as the sun, at eight in the morning, if you choose. You might, at least, forty Christmases since : but not now.

You know I must antedate my letters for special days. I am actually writing this sentence on the second December, at ten in the morning, with the feeblest possible gleam of sun on my paper ; and for the last three weeks the days have been one long drift of ragged gloom, with only sometimes five minutes' gleam of the glory of God, between the gusts, which no one regarded.

I am taking the name of God in vain, you think ? No, my religious friends, not I. For completed forty years I have been striving to consider the blue heavens, the work of His fingers, and the moon and the stars, which He hath ordained : but you have left me nothing now to consider here at Denmark Hill, but these black heavens, the work of your fingers, and the blotting of moon and stars which you have ordained ; you,—taking the name of God in vain every Sunday, and His work and His mercy in vain all the week through.

" You have nothing to do with it—you are very sorry for it—and Baron Liebig says that the power of England is coal ? "

You have everything to do with it. Were you not told to come out and be separate from all evil ? You take whatever advantage you can of the evil work and gain of this world, and yet expect the people you share with, to be damned, out of your way, in the next. If you would begin by putting them out of your way here, you would perhaps carry some of them with you there. But return to your night vision, and explain to me, if not what the angel was like, at least what you understand him to have said,—he, and those with him. With his own lips he told the shepherds there was born a Saviour for them ; but more was to be told : " And suddenly there was with him a multitude of the heavenly host."

People generally think that this verse means only that after one angel had spoken, there came more to sing, in the manner of a chorus ; but it means far another thing than that. If you look back to Genesis you find creation summed thus :—" So the heavens and earth were finished, and all the host of them." Whatever living powers of any order, great or small, were to inhabit either, are included in the word. The host of earth includes the ants and the worms of it ; the host of heaven includes,—we know not what ;—how should we ?—the creatures that are in the stars which we cannot count,—in the space which we cannot imagine ; some of them so little and so low that they can become flying poursuivants to this grain of sand we live on ; others having missions, doubtless, to larger grains of sand, and wiser creatures on them.

But the vision of their multitude means at least this ; that all the powers of the outer world which have any concern with ours became in some way visible now : having interest—they, in the praise,—as all the hosts of earth

in the life, of this Child, born in David's town. And
their hymn was of peace to the lowest of the two hosts
—peace on earth ;—and praise in the highest of the two
hosts ; and, better than peace, and sweeter than praise,
Love, among men.

The men in question, ambitious of praising God after
the manner of the hosts of heaven, have written something which they suppose this Song of Peace to have
been like: and sing it themselves, in state, after successful
battles. But you hear it, those of you who go to church
in orthodox quarters, every Sunday ; and will understand the terms of it better by recollecting that the
Lordship, which you begin the Te Deum by ascribing to
God, is this, over all creatures, or over the two Hosts.
In the Apocalypse it is " Lord, All governing "—Panto-
crator—which we weakly translate " Almighty " ; but the
Americans still understand the original sense, and apply
it so to their god, the dollar, praying that the will may
be done of their Father which is in Earth. Farther on in
the hymn, the word " Sabaoth " again means all " hosts "
or creatures ; and it is an important word for workmen
to recollect, because the saying of St. James is coming
true, and that fast, that the cries of the reapers whose
wages have been kept back by fraud, have entered into
the ears of the Lord of Sabaoth ; that is to say, Lord of
all creatures, as much of the men at St. Catherine's Docks
as of Saint Catherine herself, though they live only under
Tower-Hill, and she lived close under Sinai.

You see, farther, I have written above, not " good will towards men," but " love among men." It is nearer right so ; but the word is not easy to translate at all. What it means precisely, you may conjecture best from its use at Christ's baptism—" This is my beloved Son, in whom I am *well-pleased.*" For, in precisely the same words, the angels say, there is to be " well-pleasing in men."

Now, my religious friends, I continually hear you talk of acting for God's glory, and giving God praise. Might you not, for the present, think less of praising, and more of pleasing Him ? He can, perhaps, dispense with your praise ; your opinions of His character, even when they come to be held by a large body of the religious press, are not of material importance to Him. He has the hosts of heaven to praise Him, who see more of His ways, it is likely, than you ; but you hear that you may be pleasing to Him, if you try :—that He expected, then, to have some satisfaction in you ; and might have even great satisfaction—well-pleasing, as in His own Son, if you tried. The sparrows and the robins, if you give them leave to nest as they choose about your garden, will have their own opinions about your garden ; some of them will think it well laid out,—others ill. You are not solicitous about their opinions ; but you like them to love each other ; to build their nests without stealing each other's sticks, and to trust you to take care of them.

Perhaps, in like manner, if in this garden of the world you would leave off telling its Master your opinions of

Him, and, much more, your quarrelling about your opinions of Him ; but would simply trust Him, and mind your own business modestly, He might have more satisfaction in you than He has had yet these eighteen hundred and seventy-one years, or than He seems likely to have in the eighteen hundred and seventy-second. For first, instead of behaving like sparrows and robins, you want to behave like those birds you read the Gospel from the backs of,—eagles. Now the Lord of the garden made the claws of eagles for them, and your fingers for you ; and if you would do the work of fingers, with the fingers He made, would, without doubt, have satisfaction in you. But, instead of fingers, you want to have claws— not mere short claws, at the finger-ends, as Giotto's Injustice has them ; but long claws that will reach leagues away ; so you set to work to make yourselves manifold claws,—far-scratching ;—and this smoke, which hides the sun and chokes the sky—this Egyptian darkness that may be felt —manufactured by you, singular modern children of Israel, that you may have *no* light in your dwellings, is none the fairer, because cast forth by the furnaces, in which you forge your weapons of war.

A very singular children of Israel ! Your Father, Abraham, indeed, once saw the smoke of a country go up as the smoke of a furnace ; but not with envy of the country.

Your English power is coal ? Well ; also the power of the Vale of Siddim was in slime,—petroleum of the best ;

yet the Kings of the five cities fell there ; and the end was no well-pleasing of God among men.

Emmanuel ! God with us !—how often, you tenderly-minded Christians, have you desired to see this great sight—this Babe lying in a manger ? Yet, you have so contrived it, once more, this year, for many a farm in France, that if He were born again, in that neighbourhood, there would be found no manger for Him to lie in ; only ashes of mangers. Our clergy and lawyers dispute, indeed, whether He may not be yet among us ; if not in mangers, in the straw of them, or the corn. An English lawyer spoke twenty-six hours but the other day —the other four days, I mean—before the Lords of her Majesty's most Honourable Privy Council, to prove that an English clergyman had used a proper quantity of equivocation in his statement that Christ was in Bread. Yet there is no harm in anybody thinking that He is in Bread,—or even in Flour ! The harm is, in their expectation of His Presence in gunpowder.

Present, however, you believe He was, that night, in flesh, to any one who might be warned to go and see Him. The inn was quite full ; but we do not hear that any traveller chanced to look into the cow-house ; and most likely, even if they had, none of them would have been much interested in the workman's young wife, lying there. They probably would have thought of the Madonna, with Mr. John Stuart Mill, ('Principles of Political Economy,' 8vo, Parker, 1848, vol. ii., page 321,) that there was scarcely "any means open to her of gaining a livelihood, except as a wife and mother;" and that "women who prefer that occupation might justifiably adopt it—but, that there should be no option, no other carrière possible, for the great majority of women, except in the humbler departments of life, is one of those social injustices which call loudest for remedy."

The poor girl of Nazareth had less option than most; and with her weak "be it unto me as Thou wilt," fell so far below the modern type of independent womanhood, that one cannot wonder at any degree of contempt felt for her by British Protestants. Some few people, nevertheless, were meant, at the time, to think otherwise of her. And now, my working friends, I would ask you to read with me, carefully, for however often you may have read this before, I know there are points in the story which you have not thought of.

The shepherds were told that their Saviour was that day born to them "in David's village." We are apt to think that this was told, as of special interest to them, because David was a King.

Not so. It was told them because David was in youth *not* a King; but a Shepherd like themselves. "To you, shepherds, is born this day a Saviour in the shepherd's town;" that would be the deep sound of the message in their ears. For the great interest to them in the story of David himself must have been always, not that he had saved the monarchy, or subdued Syria, or written

Psalms, but that he had kept sheep in those very fields they were watching in ; and that his grandmother* Ruth had gone gleaning hard by.

And they said hastily, " Let us go and see."

Will you note carefully that they only think of *seeing*, not of worshipping ?   Even when they do see the Child, it is not said that they worshipped.   They were simple people, and had not much faculty of worship ; even though the heavens had opened for them, and the hosts of heaven had sung.   They had been at first only frightened ;   then curious, and communicative to the by-standers : they do not think even of making any offering, which would have been a natural thought enough, as it was to the first of shepherds : but they brought no first-lings of their flock—(it is only in pictures, and those chiefly painted for the sake of the picturesque, that the shepherds are seen bringing lambs, and baskets of eggs). It is not said here that they brought anything, but they looked, and talked, and went away praising God, as simple people,—yet taking nothing to heart ;   only the mother did that.

They went away :—"returned," it is said,—to their business, and never seem to have left it again.   Which is strange, if you think of it.   It is a good business truly, and one much to be commended, not only in itself, but as having great chances of " advancement "— as in the case of Jethro the Midianite's Jew shepherd,

---

* Great ;—father's father's mother.

and the herdsman of Tekoa ; besides the keeper of the
few sheep in the wilderness, when his brethren were
under arms afield. But why are they not seeking for
some advancement now, after opening of the heavens
to them ? or, at least, why not called to it afterwards,
being, one would have thought, as fit for ministry under
a shepherd king, as fishermen, or custom-takers ?

Can it be that the work is itself the best that can be
done by simple men ; that the shepherd Lord Clifford,
or Michael of the Green-head ghyll, are ministering better
in the wilderness than any lords or commoners are likely
to do in Parliament, or other apostleship ; so that even
the professed Fishers of Men are wise in calling themselves Pastors rather than Piscators ? Yet it seems not
less strange that one never hears of any of these shepherds any more. The boy who made the pictures in this
book for you could only fancy the Nativity, yet left his
sheep, that he might preach of it, in his way, all his life.
But they, who saw it, went back to their sheep.

Some days later, another kind of persons came. On
that first day, the simplest people of His own land ;—
twelve days after, the wisest people of other lands, far
away : persons who had received, what you are all so
exceedingly desirous to receive, a good education ; the
result of which, to you,—according to Mr. John Stuart
Mill, in the page of the chapter on the probable future
of the labouring classes, opposite to that from which I
have just quoted his opinions about the Madonna's line

of life—will be as follows :—" From this increase of intelligence, several effects may be confidently anticipated. First : that they will become even less willing than at present to be led, and governed, and directed into the way they should go, by the mere authority and prestige of superiors. If they have not now, still less will they have hereafter, any deferential awe, or religious principle of obedience, holding them in mental subjection to a class above them."

It is curious that, in this old story of the Nativity, the greater wisdom of these educated persons appears to have produced upon them an effect exactly contrary to that which you hear Mr. Stuart Mill would have " confidently anticipated." The uneducated people came only to see, but these highly trained ones to worship ; and they have allowed themselves to be led, and governed, and directed into the way which they should go, (and that a long one,) by the mere authority and prestige of a superior person, whom they clearly recognise as a born king, though not of their people. " Tell us, where is He that is born King of the Jews, for we have come to worship Him."

You may perhaps, however, think that these Magi had received a different kind of education from that which Mr. Mill would recommend, or even the book which I observe is the favourite of the Chancellor of the Exchequer—' Cassell's Educator.' It is possible ; for they were looked on in their own country as

themselves the best sort of Educators which the Cassell
of their day could provide, even for Kings. And as
you are so much interested in education, you will, perhaps, have patience with me while I translate for you a
wise Greek's account of the education of the princes
of Persia ; account given three hundred years, and more,
before these Magi came to Bethlehem.

"When the boy is seven years old he has to go and
learn all about horses, and is taught by the masters
of horsemanship, and begins to go against wild beasts ;
and when he is fourteen years old, they give him the
masters whom they call the Kingly Child-Guiders : and
these are four, chosen the best out of all the Persians
who are then in the prime of life—to wit, the most wise
man they can find, and the most just, and the most
temperate, and the most brave ; of whom the first, the
wisest, teaches the prince the magic of Zoroaster ; and
that magic is the service of the Gods : also, he teaches
him the duties that belong to a king. Then the second,
the justest, teaches him to speak truth all his life through.
Then the third, the most temperate, teaches him not to
be conquered by even so much as a single one of the
pleasures, that he may be exercised in freedom, and
verily a king, master of all things within himself, not
slave to them. And the fourth, the bravest, teaches him
to be dreadless of all things, as knowing that whenever
he fears, he is a slave."

Three hundred and some odd years before that

carpenter, with his tired wife, asked for room in the inn, and found none, these words had been written, **my** enlightened friends ; and much longer than that, these things had been done. And the three hundred and odd years (more than from Elizabeth's time till now) passed by, and much fine philosophy was talked in the interval, and many fine things found out : but it seems that when God wanted tutors for His little Prince,—at least, persons who would have been tutors to any other little prince, but could only worship this one,—He could find nothing better than those quaint-minded masters of the old Persian school. And since then, six times over, three hundred years have gone by, and we have had a good deal of theology talked in them ;—not a little popular preaching administered ; sundry Academies of studious persons assembled,—Paduan, Parisian, Oxonian, and the like ; persons of erroneous views carefully collected and burnt ; Eton, and other grammars, diligently digested ; and the most exquisite and indubitable physical science obtained,—able, there is now no doubt, to extinguish gases of every sort, and explain the reasons of their smell. And here we are, at last, finding it still necessary to treat ourselves by Cassell's Educator,—patent filter of human faculty. Pass yourselves through that, my intelligent working friends, and see how clear you will come out on the other side.

Have a moment's patience yet with me, first, while I note for you one or two of the ways of that older tutorship.

Four masters, you see, there were for the Persian Prince.
One had no other business than to teach him to speak
truth ; so difficult a matter the Persians thought it.
We know better,—we. You heard how perfectly the
French gazettes did it last year, without any tutor, by
their Holy Republican instincts. Then the second tutor
had to teach the Prince to be free. That tutor both
the French and you have had for some time back ; but
the Persian and Parisian dialects are not similar in their
use of the word " freedom " ; of that hereafter. Then
another master has to teach the Prince to fear nothing ;
him, I admit, you want little teaching from, for your
modern Republicans fear even the devil little, and God,
less ; but may I observe that you are occasionally still
afraid of thieves, though as I said some time since, I
never can make out what you have got to be stolen.

For instance, much as we suppose ourselves desirous
of beholding this Bethlehem Nativity, or getting any idea
of it, I know an English gentleman who was offered the
other day a picture of it, by a good master,—Raphael,—
for five-and-twenty pounds ; and said it was too dear :
yet had paid, only a day or two before, five hundred
pounds for a pocket-pistol that shot people out of both
ends, so afraid of thieves was he.*

None of these three masters, however, the masters of

* The papers had it that several gentlemen concurred in this piece of
business ; but they put the Nativity at five-and-twenty thousand, and the Agincourt, or whatever the explosive protector was called, at five hundred thousand.

justice, temperance, or fortitude, were sent to the little Prince at Bethlehem. Young as He was, He had already been in some practice of these; but there was yet the fourth cardinal virtue, of which, so far as we can understand, He had to learn a new manner for His new reign : and the masters of that were sent to Him— the masters of Obedience. For He had to become obedient unto Death.

And the most wise—says the Greek—the most wise master of all, teaches the boy magic; and this magic is the service of the gods.

My skilled working friends, I have heard much of your magic lately. Sleight of hand, and better than that, (you say,) sleight of machine. Léger-de-main, improved into léger-de-mécanique. From the West, as from the East, now, your American and Arabian magicians attend you ; vociferously crying their new lamps for the old stable lantern of scapegoat's horn. And for the oil of the trees of Gethsemane, your American friends have struck oil more finely inflammable. Let Aaron look to it, how he lets any run down his beard ; and the wise virgins trim their wicks cautiously, and Madeleine la Pétroleuse, with her improved spikenard, take good heed how she breaks her alabaster, and completes the worship of her Christ.

Christmas, the mass of the Lord's anointed ;—you will hear of devices enough to make it merry to you this year, I doubt not. The increase in the quantity of disposable malt liquor and tobacco is one great fact, better than all

devices. Mr. Lowe has, indeed, says the *Times* of
June 5th, "done the country good service, by placing
before it, in a compendious form, the statistics of its own
prosperity. . . . The twenty-two millions of people of
1825 drank barely nine millions of barrels of beer in
the twelve months : our thirty-two millions now living
drink all but twenty-six millions of barrels. The consumption of spirits has increased also, though in nothing
like the same proportion ; but whereas sixteen million
pounds of tobacco sufficed for us in 1825, as many as
forty-one million pounds are wanted now. By every kind
of measure, therefore, and on every principle of calcu-
lation, the growth of our prosperity is established." *

Beer, spirits, and tobacco, are thus more than ever at
your command ; and magic besides, of lantern, and harle-
quin's wand ; nay, necromancy if you will, the Witch of
Endor at number so and so round the corner, and raising
of the dead, if you roll away the tables from off them.
But of this one sort of magic, this magic of Zoroaster,
which is the service of God, you are not likely to hear.
In one sense, indeed, you have heard enough of becoming
God's servants ; to wit, servants dressed in His court
livery, to stand behind His chariot, with gold-headed
sticks. Plenty of people will advise you to apply to Him

---

* This last clause does not, you are however to observe, refer in the
great Temporal Mind, merely to the merciful Dispensation of beer and
tobacco, but to the general state of things, afterwards thus summed with
exultation : " We doubt if there is a household in the kingdom which would
now be contented with the conditions of living cheerfully accepted in 1825."

for that sort of position : and many will urge you to assist Him in carrying out His intentions, and be what the Americans call helps, instead of servants.

Well! that may be, some day, truly enough ; but before you can be allowed to help Him, you must be quite sure that you can *see* Him.   It is a question now, whether you can even see any creature of His—or the least thing that He has made,—see it,—so as to ascribe due worth, or worship to it,—how much less to its Maker ?

You have felt, doubtless, at least those of you who have been brought up in any habit of reverence, that every time when in this letter I have used an American expression, or aught like one, there came upon you a sense of sudden wrong—the darting through you of acute cold.   I meant you to feel that : for it is the essential function of America to make us all feel that.   It is the new skill they have found there ;—this skill of degradation ; others they have, which other nations had before them, from whom they have learned all they know, and among whom they must travel, still, to see any human work worth seeing. But this is their speciality, this their one gift to their race, to show men how *not* to worship,—how never to be ashamed in the presence of anything.   But the magic of Zoroaster is the exact reverse of this, to find out the worth of all things and do them reverence.

Therefore, the Magi bring treasures, as being discerners of treasures, knowing what is intrinsically worthy, and worthless ; what is best in brightness, best in sweetness, best in bitterness—gold, and frankincense, and myrrh. Finders of treasure hid in fields, and goodliness in strange pearls, such as produce no effect whatever on the public mind, bent passionately on its own fashion of pearl-diving at Gennesaret.

And you will find that the essence of the mis-teaching, of your day, concerning wealth of any kind, is in this denial of intrinsic value. What anything is worth, or not worth, it cannot tell you : all that it can tell is the exchange value. What Judas, in the present state of Demand and Supply, can get for the article he has to sell, in a given market, that is the value of his article :— Yet you do not find that Judas had joy of his bargain. No Christmas, still less Easter, holidays, coming to him with merrymaking. Whereas, the Zoroastrians, who " take stars for money," rejoice with exceeding great joy at seeing something, which—they cannot put in their pockets. For, " the vital principle of their religion is the recognition of one supreme power ; the God of Light— in every sense of the word—the Spirit who creates the world, and rules it, and defends it against the power of evil." *

I repeat to you, now, the question I put at the beginning of my letter. What is this Christmas to you ? What Light is there, for your eyes, also, pausing yet over the place where the Child lay?

I will tell you, briefly, what Light there should be ;—

* MAX MÜLLER : 'Genesis and the Zend-Avesta.'

what lessons and promise are in this story, at the least. There may be infinitely more than I know ; but there is certainly, this.

The Child is born to bring you the promise of new life. Eternal or not, is no matter ; pure and redeemed, at least.

He is born twice on your earth ; first, from the womb, to the life of toil ; then, from the grave, to that of rest.

To His first life He is born in a cattle-shed, the supposed son of a carpenter ; and afterwards brought up to a carpenter's craft.

But the circumstances of His second life are, in great part, hidden from us : only note this much of it. The three principal appearances to His disciples are accompanied by giving or receiving of food. He is known at Emmaus in breaking of bread ; at Jerusalem He Himself eats fish and honey to show that He is not a spirit ; and His charge to Peter is " when they had dined," the food having been obtained under His direction.

But in His first showing Himself to the person who loved Him best, and to whom He had forgiven most, there is a circumstance more singular and significant still. Observe—assuming the accepted belief to be true,—this was the first time when the Maker of men showed Himself to human eyes, risen from the dead, to assure them of immortality. You might have thought He would have shown Himself in some brightly glorified form,—in some sacred and before unimaginable beauty.

He shows Himself in so simple aspect, and dress, that she, who, of all people on the earth, should have known Him best, glancing quickly back through her tears, does not know Him. Takes Him for " the gardener."

Now, unless absolute orders had been given to us, such as would have rendered error impossible, (which would have altered the entire temper of Christian probation) ; could we possibly have had more distinct indication of the purpose of the Master—borne first by witness of shepherds, in a cattle-shed, then by witness of the person for whom He had done most, and who loved Him best, in the garden, and in gardener's guise, and not known even by His familiar friends till He gave them bread— could it be told us, I repeat, more definitely by any sign or indication whatsoever, that the noblest human life was appointed to be by the cattle-fold and in the garden ; and to be known as noble in breaking of bread ?

Now, but a few words more. You will constantly hear foolish and ignoble persons conceitedly proclaiming the text, that " not many wise and not many noble are called."

Nevertheless, of those who are truly wise, and truly noble, all are called that exist. And to sight of this Nativity, you find that, together with the simple persons, near at hand, there were called precisely the wisest men that could be found on earth at that moment.

And these men, for their own part, came—I beg you

very earnestly again to note this—not to see, nor talk —but to do reverence. They are neither curious nor talkative, but submissive.

And, so far as they came to teach, they came as teachers of one virtue only: Obedience. For of this Child, at once Prince and Servant, Shepherd and Lamb, it was written: " See, mine elect, in whom my soul delighteth. He shall not strive, nor cry, till he shall bring forth Judgment unto Victory."

My friends, of the black country, you **may** have wondered at my telling you so often,—I tell you nevertheless, once more, in bidding you farewell this year,—that one main purpose of the education I want you to seek is, that you **may** see the sky, with the stars of it again ; and be enabled, in their material light—" riveder le stelle."

But, much more, out of this blackness of the smoke of the Pit, the blindness of heart, in which the children of *Dis*obedience blaspheme God and each other, heaven grant to you the vision of that sacred light, at pause over the place where the young Child was laid ; and ordain that more and more in each coming Christmas it may be said of you, " When they saw the Star, they rejoiced with exceeding great joy."

Believe me your faithful servant,

JOHN RUSKIN.